"I like this book because it encourages parents to come along for the ride and learn about investing, too."

   —Money.com

"In-depth and sophisticated...[*TeenVestor*®] doesn't assume its readers have had prior exposure to investing or easy access to money...Teens and parents will appreciate the detailed treatment of investing strategies."

   —Morningstar.com

"The authors explain the basics of investing...how to understand the stock market, and how to evaluate and choose stocks for the long-term...Accurate, objective, and helpful."

   —*School Library Journal*

"Psst. Find this website on the Internet and bookmark it. *TeenVestor.com*. Just don't let anyone know you're using it. It's supposed to be for kids. If you want to learn about investing, this is the place to go. It's for teens, but if you won't tell, we won't either. This is good stuff."

   —*Independent Tribune*

"Both the book and the website are clearly laid out and offer good information in an accessible, and unlike many books aimed toward the younger market, unpatronizing manner...Most teens are not old enough to invest through a regular investment account, so there's a chapter going through the options open to parents of teens, such as custodial account and IRAs."

   —FinancialFinesse.com

TEENVESTOR

**The Practical Investment
Guide for Teens and
Their Parents**

Emmanuel Modu and Andréa Walker

A PERIGEE BOOK

A Perigee Book
Published by The Berkley Publishing Group
A division of Penguin Putnam Inc.
375 Hudson Street
New York, New York 10014

Previously published by Gateway Publishers
First Perigee edition: January 2002

Published simultaneously in Canada.

Visit our website at www.penguinputnam.com

Library of Congress Cataloging-in-Publication Data

Modu, Emmanuel.
    [Teenvestor.com]
    Teenvestor: the practical investment guide for teens and their parents /Emmanuel
Modu, Andrea Walker.
       p. cm.
    Originally published: Teenvestor.com Newark, N.J.:Gateway Publishers, 2000.
    Includes index.
    ISBN 0-399-52760-5
    1. Teenagers—Finance, Personal. 2. Investments. 3. Finance, Personal.
    I. Walker, Andrea. II. Title

                    HG179. M566 2001
                    332.6'0835—dc21

         Printed in the United States of America
              10 9 8 7 6 5 4 3 2 1

TABLE OF CONTENTS

ACKNOWLEDGMENTS

From the beginning, *TeenVestor* has been a family endeavor. Thanks to our parents, siblings, and children for their unwavering support of our work.

We dedicate this book to the next group of Teenvestors in our lives:

Nkem, Amara, Ikenna, Ije, Anziya, and Eugenia.

Our sincere thanks to our agent, Jane Jordan Browne, and Scott Mendel of Multimedia Product Development, Inc., and our editor at Perigee Books, Jennifer Repo.

INTRODUCTION I
(FOR TEENVESTORS®)

You are holding in your hands the first investment book written especially for teenagers and their parents. No other book thoroughly covers the practical nuts and bolts of investing in a manner the young can easily understand. In addition, www.teenvestor.com, the book's companion website, is full of information to make you a smarter and more prudent investor.

Once you start learning how to invest, you will be transformed from a teenager to a Teenvestor®. A Teenvestor is anyone between the ages of 13 and 19 interested in investing in stocks, mutual funds, starting a business, education, or in anything else that will improve his well-being.

Most aspiring Teenvestors have neither the money nor the time necessary to become millionaires overnight in the stock and mutual fund markets. With a bit of knowledge, however, Teenvestors could make a good amount of money if they steadily invest in good companies over a long period of time. Over time, you too can start putting your money away in strong companies and be well ahead of your peers, financially.

It is easy to get wrong ideas about how money is made in the stock market if you listen to the news or read the headlines. The media would have you believe that the stock market is just giving away money. Sure, we know you've heard stories of people getting rich by buying Internet stocks. Yes, some people have indeed made money in those types of fast-growing technology stocks, but many have also lost money by buying high and then watching their share prices fall to new lows. Just don't believe all the hype.

No one is born with the knowledge of how to invest. Some people try to learn investing by just diving into stocks or mutual funds without understanding the basics. Of course, when they try to learn investing this way, they can lose their savings quickly. You, on the other hand, are lucky enough to be living at a time when you can easily get the basic knowledge to become a good, steady investor.

What are the advantages of learning how to invest at a young age? First, you will get a jump-start on all your peers. While your friends are worrying about affording new in-line skates, you will be investing in their manufacturer. While your classmates are setting aside their holiday gift money for a new computerized gadget, you will be stashing money away for the future when, hopefully, you'll accumulate enough cash by selling your stocks or mutual funds for a new car, computer, your education, and other items that will last a lot longer than those gadgets.

Investment principles learned at an early age will stay with you forever. When you start to appreciate how money grows by earning interest on interest (also known as *compounding*) and by investing long-term in stocks and mutual funds, you will realize that a little money invested today, can produce much more tomorrow.

WHY INVEST IN THE STOCK MARKET

For most people, investment choices include stocks (and stock mutual funds), corporate bonds, and government bonds. Stocks, as you may already know, represent how much of a company an investor owns. Corporate bonds are loans investors make to corporations, and government bonds are loans investors make to the government.

Investing in the stock market, statistics show us, has earned investors an average of 11.2% profit each year for the past 72 years or so. This is far more than the 5.8% average yearly profit for long-term corporate bonds, and more than the 5.3% average yearly profit for government bonds in the same 72-year period. What this says is that stocks are better than other investments if you are a long-term investor. By owning stocks you will be in good company because 80 million Americans own stocks at this time.

YOUR ONE BIG ADVANTAGE

As an investor, you have one big advantage over your parents and other adults—time. The younger you are, the more time you have to invest, and this gives your investments time to grow through the power of *compounding*. Compounding, as we will discuss more fully in the book, is the idea that if you make a habit of reinvesting any profit you earn on your investments back into your original investment, your money will multiply before you know it. A simple example would be a $1,000 yearly deposit in a bank account (paying a 10% each year in interest) for the next 50 years. If the depositor reinvested every penny of interest back into the account, she would have $1,280,349 at the end of the 50th year. If you just summed up the amount of money she would have saved if she stuffed the money into a giant piggy bank, she would have only $50,000 (50 years x $1,000 = $50,000). Yes, we know you can't even think about your life that far in the future. However, we are trying to illustrate how steady investing over a long period of time can make your money multiply. And at your age, you have the time.

THE FORMAT AND CONVENTIONS IN THIS BOOK

This book is written primarily for Teenvestors, but it contains three chapters written specifically for parents: Introduction II, Chapter 2 (Helping Teenvestors Manage Money), and Chapter 21 (Taxes and Tax-Friendly Investments). We recommend that your parents also read Chapter 20 (Online Brokers) and Chapter 22 (The Teenvestor Ten), even though they are written for Teenvestors, so they can help you establish an account with a company that will assist you in buying and selling stocks and mutual funds.

This book concentrates on teaching Teenvestors how to invest in the stocks of America's biggest and most profitable companies. We also touch upon other investments related to stocks such as mutual funds and special bonds that are appropriate for young investors.

At times, we repeat certain important concepts. This is deliberate because certain ideas need to be repeated with examples Teenvestors can relate to.

You will also notice that we use both pronouns "he" and "she." This too, is deliberate because we feel that both male and female Teenvestors should feel comfortable reading the book and relating to its contents.

In addition, some of the topics discussed in this book are for the advanced Teenvestor—a Teenvestor who is at least 15 years old and who has been investing for two years or more. The average reader can skip these sections and still understand the ideas in the remainder of the book.

On our website, www.teenvestor.com, you will find additional information about the topics covered in each chapter. In addition, you will find answers to the chapter assignments that help emphasize the investment concepts in the book. By the time you complete these assignments, you will know more about investing than most college graduates and the average adult.

Teenvestor: The Practical Investment Guide for Teens and their Parents and its accompanying website should be the first stop for any young person who wants to gain investment skills that will last a lifetime. No one can learn all they need to know about investing from one source but this book can give you a jump-start. Just read patiently, use the information resources we provide, and begin investing in solid companies right away!

INTRODUCTION II
(FOR PARENTS)

Teenvestor: The Practical Investment Guide for Teens and their Parents is our solution to the lack of investment education necessary to teach the very young how to become lifelong investors. The word *Teenvestor*®, used throughout this book, refers to anyone between the ages of 13 and 19 interested in investing in stocks, mutual funds, starting a business, education, or in anything else that will improve his well-being. In this book, we'll concentrate on teaching Teenvestors how to invest primarily in the stock and mutual fund markets. Along with a companion website, www.teenvestor.com, *Teenvestor* breaks new ground in that it considers investment education as the normal part of the education process of young people.

Teenvestor was written with the understanding that the young need survival skills different from those required just 30 years ago. They face the prospect of diminished social safety nets (such as reduced Social Security benefits and welfare), the prospect of managing more of their retirement funds on their own, and the likelihood that they will have to shoulder more of their own educational and medical expenses as the government and companies find new ways to implement budget cuts. These realities make it imperative that children learn ways to make their money grow, no matter how small the initial amount. By exposing their children to stocks, mutual funds, and other financial instruments at an early age, parents lay the foundation for their children to become savvy adult investors.

PARENTAL HOPES AND DREAMS

Some parents today recognize that their children should learn how to save and invest. More than ever before, they are concerned about their children's financial future, and they realize that reading, 'riting and 'rithmetic are no longer sufficient to guarantee a decent standard of living. Indeed, financial experts agree that young people need financial skills to survive the economic challenges of their adulthood.

The desire on the part of some parents to teach their children about investing has not gone unnoticed by brokerage firms. A number of companies are moving to capture the potential investing power in this country and, thereby, to expand their market reach to a new group of investors with whom they can build a long-term relationship.

The Stein Roe Young Investors Fund, a $993 million-dollar mutual fund specifically marketed to young investors, lists young-investor education as one of its goals in its prospectus. Another fund, the USAA First Start Growth Fund, also appeals to young investors and goes as far as to take investment ideas from them.

The popularity of these funds shows that there is demand for investments the young can understand, and some companies are capitalizing on the desire of parents to teach their children investment basics.

HISTORICAL LACK OF INVESTMENT EDUCATION

Unfortunately, not all parents appreciate the need to help their children become Teenvestors or can easily find age-appropriate help for their children. If you do have a slight interest in boosting your children's financial acumen, you probably won't get much help from the educational institutions your children attend. It appears that many school systems make a point of avoiding the topic of teaching the young how to handle money. It is odd that a country with the largest gross national product in the world produces graduates who know very little about money and how to make it grow.

REASONS PARENTS DON'T ENCOURAGE
YOUNG INVESTORS

Investing is a good habit that can be learned at an early age. Regular investors end up saving far more than occasional investors even when they regularly invest a small amount at a time. The most important thing about investing, however, is that time is your friend—the earlier a person starts, the better off that person will be in the long run. And time is a good friend of Teenvestors, most of whom will retire in about 51 years.

Unfortunately, however, the typical investor is a 45-year-old man. What about all those with the power of youth behind them? Why shouldn't young people learn that they too can make their money grow? As with most things in life, parents have a big influence on their children's savings and investment habits. Parents are the ones that have to step up and introduce their children to the lifelong journey of money management.

In our research, we have found that there are five major reasons parents shy away from encouraging their children to start investing at an early age: (1) Parents themselves don't know much about investing; (2) Parents think their children can't understand investing concepts; (3) Parents fear their children might put too much emphasis on money; (4) Parents think that teaching their children about investing will interfere with their basic education (like the three R's); and (5) Parents think investing skills will come naturally with maturity.

Parents Themselves Don't Know Much About Investing

Some parents just don't know much about investing. To many of them, investing money can be quite confusing and intimidating. For one thing, it looks so mysterious. All that jargon such as earnings per share, leverage, price-earning ratios, dividend yields, and others is enough to intimidate any individual looking for a basic understanding of investments. Then there is the myth that investing requires great mathematical acumen. With all these perceived barriers to becoming an investor, many people choose to stay out of the markets completely or let the "experts" handle their money, at a great expense, we might add. But what you don't know is that many brokers don't have more than high school diplomas. What they do have, however, is the benefit of experience; experience they gain by essentially advising you on what stocks, bonds, and mutual funds you should buy.

One of the problems with turning everything over to the so-called financial experts is that you don't learn anything about investing. What this means is that you will always be dependent on brokers who are probably no smarter than you are. It also means that you have no knowledge about investing that you can pass onto your children (except perhaps, to advise them to get a broker). But an old African proverb says: "A man's morning begins whenever he wakes up during the day." Translation: it is never too late to wake up and start changing your attitudes and behavior. Starting with this book, you can learn investment basics so you can help your children become Teenvestors.

Parents Think Their Children Can't Understand Investing Concepts

Most of you have probably heard of Junior Achievement, which for the past 70 years has been teaching children about capitalism—including the stock market. However, you may not know of other organizations such as The Security Industry Associate (which runs The Stock Market Game, a contest for aspiring young investors), Young Americans Education Foundation, Teen Business Camp, The National Council on Economic Education, The JumpStart Coalition for Personal Financial Literacy, and many more that have been successful at teaching young people about money and investment basics. These organizations have been quietly getting young people prepared for a money-savvy life. See our website, www.teenvestor.com, for a list of organizations that teach young people about money and investing.

We have personally experienced the ease with which young people can pick up clearly presented investment concepts. For years, we ran Teen Business Camp in which 14- to 17-year olds spent 2 weeks on a college campus to learn about the stock market and entrepreneurship. One year we established a stock portfolio with Merrill Lynch & Co. and tracked the results daily, noting any economic news that affected the portfolio. The Teenvestors graduated from the program with a working knowledge of the stock market—much more knowledge than an average 21-year-old college graduate's.

Parents Fear Their Children Might Put Too Much Emphasis On Money

Some parents avoid teaching investing at an early age because they fear that their Teenvestors will put too much value on making money. To ensure that Teenvestors establish healthy money habits without being obsessed with money, parents should continue the moral lessons they teach daily. Teaching your Teenvestors investment concepts is only one of the ways to insure that they are prepared for a more financially stressful life when they reach adulthood. The reality is that your children will have to learn about money one way or another, with or without your help. You can make sure they put money and investing in perspective—neither making it the most important thing in their lives nor ignoring the benefits of saving and investing. Without your help, they will grow up unprepared for financial difficulties they may face at some point in their lives.

Parents Think That Teaching Their Children About Investing Will Interfere With Their Basic Education

Some parents think that teaching their children investment basics will interfere with the three R's—reading, 'riting and 'rithmetic. We believe that investment skills are as important as the basic academic skills students learn in school. We hold this view because of the vast changes in the American economy in the past few decades. For one, stability in the workforce has disappeared. There are no more job guarantees and this means that, as adults, your children may face financial droughts unless they know how to save and invest their hard-earned money. In addition, consider these possibilities: young people face the prospects of receiving less financial aid for their education, diminished social safety nets (such as reduced Social Security benefits and welfare), managing more of their retirement funds on their own than you do now, and of shouldering more of their own medical expenses. These realities make it imperative that your children learn more than how to read, write, and do calculus. They also have to know about growing whatever amount of money they have.

Parents Think Investing Skills Will Come Naturally With Maturity

Hoping that the young will pick up investment skills as they get older is wishful thinking. We firmly believe that money management skills are similar to other skills such as learning how to play tennis or the piano. Children don't just magically know how to play tennis by watching Wimbledon. They have to hammer away at the ball on the court under the watchful eye of someone who can teach them how to swing. Golf superstar Tiger Woods started swinging golf clubs at the age of four. There is no question that the earlier one begins to learn a skill, the better. In addition, if you let your children learn how to manage money by trial and error, they may never learn that saving and investing should be a lifelong habit.

ENCOURAGING GIRLS TO INVEST

For parents of daughters, we have a special message: Don't shortchange them when it comes to instruction about money and investing. Gone are the days when girls waited for Mr. Right to marry them and support them forever. The truth is that today's women (yes, even your grown-up little girl) may stay single longer, have their own careers, outlive their husbands (if they marry), and get divorced. In addition, because money can be a source of control and power, it is necessary that women know how to manage and invest it. Teaching girls about investing will help them face challenges and opportunities encountered by women in our society.

If we haven't yet convinced you about the importance of teaching your girls about investing, keep in mind that some of the best financial experts on Wall Street are women. Abby Joseph Cohen, co-chair of the Goldman Sachs Investment Policy Committee, can actually move the financial markets when she issues her opinions. Mary Farrell, managing director at Paine Webber, is another woman of Wall Street whose opinions are greatly valued by investors. Mary Meeker, Morgan Stanley Dean Witter's Internet analyst, is yet another highly respected female voice on Wall Street. There are so many influential women on Wall Street that we can't list them all here. For more information on this subject, *Women Of The Street* by Sue Herrera (a leading financial journalist) describes the stellar careers of some of the female financial experts who are great at what they do.

Beyond Wall Street, there are plenty of examples of women who have demonstrated the business and financial savvy to run large companies. The following executives come to mind: Hewlett-Packard CEO Carly Fiorina, eBay CEO Meg Whitman, Avon CEO Andrea Jung and Oglivy and Mather CEO Shelly Lazarus. These women, together with "women of the Street," can serve as role models for your Teenvestors.

There are programs such as Camp Startup, Club Invest, Financial Camp For Girls, and Girls Inc., which specialize in teaching investing to girls. These along with general business magazines we discuss in chapter 11 should help you get your Teenvestors going. You can also find a list of publications and organizations, complete with links, on our website, www.teenvestor.com.

ENCOURAGING MINORITIES TO INVEST

A study of 4,309 families commissioned by the U.S. Federal Reserve found that minority families (i.e., Hispanics, African-Americans, Asians, and others) have a median net worth of $16,400 while white families have a median net worth of $94,900—a gap of $78,500. Because net worth includes the value of owned assets such as stocks, homes, cars, and bank accounts, this gap is much wider than the income gap of about $14,400—the difference between $37,700 median income for whites and $23,300 median income for minorities. While there are social reasons why the wealth gap is so wide, one of the major contributors to this gap is the lack of minority participation in the stock market. For example, New York University Economics Professor Edward Wolff tells *The Wall Street Journal* that only 10.7% of blacks owned stock as opposed to 48% of whites that owned stock during the economic expansion of the 90s.

Furthermore, with regard to African-Americans, a survey commissioned by Chicago-based Ariel Mutual Funds and conducted by pollster Roper Starch Worldwide, polled about 500 African-Americans and 500 non–African-Americans with income over $30,000. The survey revealed that while African-Americans expected a yield of 14.7% on their investment choices, non–African-Americans wanted a yield of 11.2%. The catch was that even though African-Americans expected higher yields on their investments, they were less likely to invest in stocks and mutual funds— the investment vehicles that are necessary to achieve such returns. Says Ariel President John Rogers, "African Americans are often inhibited from plunging into the stock market because many of our parents and grandparents were not involved in investing."

If you are a minority, starting your children early on an investment track can help them feel more comfortable in putting their money in stocks—one of the best assets for building wealth in the long run.

African-American parents can point their Teenvestors to some prominent Wall Street and business role models such as: Kenneth I. Chenault who is now the President, Chairman and CEO of American Express Company; Stanley E. O'Neal, President of Merrill Lynch & Co.'s influential Private Client Group, who is in contention for the CEO position; Franklin D. Raines who is the Chairman and CEO of Fannie Mae, the largest non-bank financial services company in the world; Reginald F. Lewis, the deceased CEO of the now-dismembered TLC Beatrice International Holdings, Inc., who built a billion-dollar business empire; and Kim Goodwin, Chief Investment Officer of U.S. Growth Equities at American Century Investment Management, Inc., who leads the team that manages about $60 billion in domestic growth funds.

If you are a Hispanic parent, you should know that your children have plenty of well-respected business leaders to look up to. Under the presidency of Richard E. Rivera, Red Lobster has surpassed sales of $2 billion for the first time in its 33-year history. Another savvy industry leader is Carlos Gutierrez, Chairman and CEO of the giant cereal maker, Kellog — a company with nearly $7 billion in sales. Internet pioneer Julio Gomez provides yet another example of a successful Hispanic businessman. Mr. Gomez, the CEO of Gomez Advisors came up with the idea of a website to rank online products and services. According to *Time* magazine, he is one of the top visionaries shaping technology today. There are countless other Hispanics in various positions of leadership and in a wide variety of industries that can serve as role models for your Teenvestors.

We recommend that you start looking for role models in some of the general business publications we list in Chapter 11. You can also find a list of publications and organizations, complete with links, on our website, www.teenvestor.com.

THE BEST INVESTMENT FOR TEENVESTORS

Now that we have convinced you that teaching your children how to invest is important, what type of investment should they make with their money? The typical investor has three investment choices: stocks (including his employer's investment incentives), corporate bonds, and government bonds. (Mutual funds are largely made up of a combination of stocks and bonds).

Historically, stocks have had an advantage over corporate bonds and government bonds. For the past 72 years, stocks, corporate bonds, and government bonds have returned an average of 11.2%, 5.8%, and 5.3%, respectively. More than 80 million people in the United States participate in the stock market in one way or another.

While there are no foolproof investments, investing in the stock market is more profitable and more appropriate for children than is investing in bonds, real estate, and other assets that require a lot of money.

YOUR RESPONSIBILITY AS THE PARENT OF A TEEN-VESTOR

The year 2000 was a landmark year in the life of Teenvestors. In that year, the Securities and Exchange Commission (SEC), the watchdog of the financial markets, brought a fraud case against a 15-year-old boy named Jonathan Lebed. It was the first such case ever brought against a teenager. The SEC accused Jonathan of using the Internet to "pump and dump" the stocks of small companies that he had previously purchased. According to the SEC, Jonathan used the Internet to spread false or misleading information about the prospects of these companies (i.e. pumped the stocks). As a result of the fraudulent promotion of these companies, the prices of the stocks went up when people who believed Jonathan's glowing remarks bought the stocks. The SEC alleged that once the stock prices increased, Jonathan then sold his shares (i.e. dumped the stocks), netting over $800,000 in the process. Jonathan settled the case with the SEC without agreeing or disagreeing with the charges. The case received considerable press and underscores the need for parents to supervise their Teenvestor's investment activities. Here are some basic guidelines for you and your Teenvestor:

1. *Make your teenvestor aware of the law.* Before your teen starts investing, make sure she knows some of the basic rules governing what she can or cannot do as an investor. One thing she is not supposed to do is to establish an online trading account on her own. Although we recognize that it is possible for her to open an account on her own, because of the anonymity of the Internet, we strongly advise against it be-

cause it is illegal. Under the law, she can only trade stocks through a custodial account that you establish on her behalf and that you control. (See chapter 21 for information on custodial accounts.) Another restriction that your Teenvestor must understand is that she can't profit from any important non-public information about a publicly traded company. This means, for example, that she can't invest in shares of your employer's stock on the basis of valuable confidential information she learned from you at the dinner table. Finally, as evidenced by the Jonathan Lebed case, she can't engage in "pump and dump" schemes. (You can get more information about investment rules and regulations from the SEC's excellent website, www.sec.gov.)

2. *Establish moral/ethical ground rules*. As a parent, you can't avoid your responsibility in terms of establishing guidelines about the type of companies in which your Teenvestor can invest. In our opinion, ethical and moral considerations should not go out the window when it comes to investing. For example, if you are morally opposed to gambling, your Teenvestor should not invest in gaming establishments. If you have a problem with companies that make tobacco products, you should impose a ban on the stocks of such business enterprises. In short, whenever possible and practical, there should be some consistency in the moral and ethical lessons you are teaching you children in the normal course of life and the investment lessons they learn as Teenvestors.

3. *Ban investments in penny stocks*. Your Teenvestor should avoid "penny stocks." These are stocks of very tiny companies and, as you can tell by the name, the stocks usually trade for pennies. It is through penny stocks that stock investment scam artists typically hook unsuspecting investors. Keep in mind that there is nothing necessarily wrong with companies that issue these stocks. The problem is that because there are usually very few publicly available documents to give investors reliable information about the health of these companies, unscrupulous brokers and advisors can easily lure naïve investors to purchase their stocks. The SEC's case against Jonathan Lebed involved the allegation that he distributed false or exaggerated claims about penny stocks.

4. *Discourage the use of chat rooms for investment information*. Your Teenvestor should avoid getting investment information from Internet chat rooms—especially information about small companies whose financial data is hard to verify. Chatters have been known for churning out false information and your Teenvestor may not have the ability to sift out the good information from the bad. There are plenty of investment research sites that can help your Teenvestor determine in which companies to invest. (See chapter 22 and our website, www.teenvestor.com, for more information.)

5. *Supervise your teenvestor's trading activities*. Because you will be the custodian of you Teenvestor's investment account, the statements from online brokers will come to you. You should pay attention to transactions on the statements to make

sure that she is following whatever guidelines you have set in terms of permissible investments, investment size and investment frequency.

HOW TO USE THIS BOOK

This book is written primarily for Teenvestors, but it contains three chapters written specifically for you: this introductory chapter, chapter 2 ("Helping Teenvestors Manage Money"), and chapter 21 ("Taxes and Tax-Friendly Investments"). We recommend, also, that you read chapter 20 ("Online Brokers") and chapter 22 ("The Teenvestor Ten") so you can help your Teenvestor choose and establish an online trading account. If you are a novice investor yourself, perhaps you should read the entire book so you can better help your Teenvestor and yourself.

The book concentrates on teaching Teenvestors how to invest in the stock of America's biggest companies. We also touch upon other investments related to stocks such as mutual funds. In addition, we mention how Teenvestors can invest in CDs and zero-coupon bonds (which include U.S. Savings Bonds).

In some sections of the book, we point your Teenvestor to our website, www.teenvestor.com, for more details about the ideas we are teaching them. On our website, they will also find links to other good investment websites.

Some sections of the book have assignments that your Teenvestor should complete and the solutions to the assignments are contained on our site. When she completes these assignments, your Teenvestor will know more about investing than most college graduates and even some graduates with MBAs.

1

GETTING AND MANAGING MONEY

Advising Teenvestors on how to invest without telling them how to get money to do so is pointless. In this chapter, we explore your choices on getting and saving money to put in stocks, mutual funds, or any other financial investment.

You have only three ways to get the money you need for investing: you can get money from your parents and relatives, from a job, and from your own business. We will discuss these three options in this chapter.

MONEY FROM PARENTS AND RELATIVES

Many of the Teenvestors we've met get most of their investment money from their parents and relatives. This money includes cash gifts, allowance, and money for certain chores done around the house. If you receive no regular allowance from your parents, you can start campaigning now for one. But you should show that you can be responsible with the money they give you. To prove to them that you can handle money responsibly, we have some suggestions for you.

Propose An Allowance Figure

You can show you're serious about saving and investing by proposing an allowance figure. If you currently receive an allowance, the technique we suggest will make sure the amount is appropriate for your needs. Forget about telling your parents about your friend's big allowance. That technique won't work. The only thing that will work is for you to carefully think about your own needs and match them with the amount you are requesting.

Before you can propose an allowance figure (and be on your way to becoming a good Teenvestor), you must learn how to create a *budget*. A budget is a way to show how you spend or save the money you get each week or month from your parents, relatives, a job, or other sources such as your own business.

The Family Budget

Your parents may create a budget for your family each month. If so, your family's budget will include your parents' total monthly salary and expenses such as rent or *mortgage* (payments on your parents' house loan) and other items. Table 1.1 on the next page shows an example of a family's monthly budget. Notice that the first item on the table is *income*, or the money the family keeps after paying taxes on its salary.

TABLE 1.1
Monthly Budget Example For A Family

Income
   1. Monthly Salary (after taxes) $4,200

     TOTAL INCOME   **$4,200**

Expenses

1.	Rent or Mortgage	$900
2.	Electricity/Gas/Oil	$200
3.	Telephone	$100
4.	Water	$30
5.	Property Tax	$100
6.	Household Items	$150
7.	Food	$800
8.	Car Payments	$350
9.	Car Insurance	$70
10.	Education For Children	$400
11.	Credit Card Payments	$200
12.	Savings & Investments	$400
13.	Gifts	$100
14.	Recreation	$100
15.	Vacation Money	$200
16.	Other	$100

     TOTAL EXPENSES   **$4,200**

Expense items 1 to 11 on Table 1.1 are some of the expenses that most families must pay each month. If the family does not pay its rent or mortgage it will find itself homeless. If the family does not make its credit card payments, it will find that credit card companies will be calling to demand payment.

The next expense item on the list (expense item 12) is "Savings & Investments." Experts recommend that each family should always put money aside for savings and investments after "must-pay" bills such as mortgage and rent are taken care of. These experts call the act of setting aside savings and investment amounts as "paying yourself first."

After Savings & Investments, you will see other expenses that are somewhat less important than the others.

Items such as gifts, recreation, and vacation are nice but they can be eliminated from the budget if the family needs extra money immediately. These types of expenses are called *discretionary expenses*. Eliminating gifts, for example, may make family members unhappy, but it may be necessary if a parent loses his or her job.

Some expenses are not monthly expenses. For example, some families put aside money each month for a once-a-year vacation. They spread out this once-a-year expense over a 12-month period to avoid having to come up with a lump sum for a vacation. As an example, let's say that a vacation will cost a family $2,400. This means that if the family has a whole year to put aside money each month for the trip, $200 will have to be put aside each month. The calculation is as follows:

Monthly Amount = Amount / (#Of Months To Pay For It)

In our example, the "Amount" is $2,400, and the "# Of Months To Pay For It" is the number of months the family will save before accumulating enough cash for the trip—12 months. The "Monthly Amount" is then equal to:

$2,400 / 12 months = $200 per month

The numbers on Table 1.1 won't match what your parents make or spend but the table itself will show some of the categories of expenses your parents may have to meet each month. By the way, not all parents like to tell their children exactly how much they make or spend.

ASSIGNMENT 1.1

Write down the major categories of expenses you believe your parents pay every month. Then talk to them to see what items you may be missing.

Your Own Budget

One thing always holds true for budgets: money that comes into your hands (or income) should be equal to the money you spend paying for things and on "Savings & Investments". The equation can be written like this:

Money You Get = Money You Spend On Paying For Things
+ Money Set Aside For "Savings & Investments"

Your first step is to write down all the things you spend money on and the things your parents buy for you. These items should fall into three groups:

1. Small items that you buy or pay for on a weekly basis like school lunches, snacks, or bus money. If you pay for some of these items daily, add them up to show the weekly amount.

2. Small amounts you ask from your parents for leisure activities or hobbies such as going to the movies, to the skating rink, video game arcade, etc.

3. Purchases such as shoes, clothes, software and other big-ticket items that you or your parents pay for every once in a while.

Worksheet 1.1 on the next page is for you to write down your weekly income and weekly expenses. This should include the items in groups 1 and 2. If you are also responsible for buying items in group 3, include it as well.

On the income side, you have several ways of getting money: from parents and relatives, from a job, or from a business you run.

Unlike the family budget, your personal budget should be for weekly amounts. You can also prepare a worksheet for monthly expenses if you'd like, but we think that weekly is the way to go because most parents give weekly allowances to their children.

Make sure that each item you put on the worksheet is reasonable. Remember that you will use this worksheet to ask your parents for a fair allowance if they can afford to give you money each week.

The purpose of creating this budget is to show your parents that you are serious about handling more of your own expenses. This is a very important step because before your parents can trust you with more cash, they have to be sure that you can budget your own money wisely. Notice that the third expense item on Worksheet 1.1 is "Savings & Investments." Once again, savings and investments should be listed after the items that a person must pay for first. Please don't ever put savings and investing last on your list. We think it belongs close

---

Worksheet 1.1
Weekly Budget Example For Teenvestors

Income
1. Money From Parents $
2. Money From Relatives $
3. Money From A Job $
4. Money From A Business $

   TOTAL INCOME $

Expenses
1. School Lunch $
2. Other School Items $

3. Savings & Investments $

4. Daily Newspaper $
5. Gas (if you drive) $
6. Magazine Subscriptions $
7. Snacks $

8.   Long-Term Goal $
9.   Short-Term Goal $
10. Other Item #1 $
11. Other Item #2 $
12. Other Item #3 $
13. Other Item #4 $
14. Other Item #5 $

   TOTAL EXPENSES $

---

to the top for teens since their parents provide most of the things they need for survival, like rent or food.

The two lines, "Long-Term Goal" and "Short-Term Goal" (expense lines number 8 and 9), need explanations. A *goal* is something you are trying to achieve. For example, your goal for the next two weeks could be to read a book cover-to-cover. Your parents' goal could be to learn Italian for a vacation in Europe next year.

You can have social goals (such as learning a language), political goals (such as becoming your class president), educational goals (college), financial goals (such as investing in stocks within one month), and other goals. In this book, of course, we are concentrating on financial goals.

You can have long-term goals or short-term goals. Long-term goals are things you want to accomplish in a year or two or more. Short-term goals are things you want to accomplish in a matter of days, weeks, or months.

Your budget already includes your savings and investment goals. But what about goals to buy a computer or a special electronic game? A computer costing a few hundred dollars will probably be considered a long-term goal. A game will probably be in the short-term-goal category unless it costs over $50 or so.

If, for example, you want to spend no more than $1,000 for a computer, you may have to spread the purchase over one year to save enough to buy it. To get the weekly amount you would have to save, divide $1,000 by the 52 weeks in a year. This amounts to:

$$\$1,000 / 52 \text{ weeks} = \$19.23 \text{ per week}$$

So on your weekly budget, you should insert $19.23 per week in the Long-Term Goal line (expense line 8). If you create a monthly budget instead of a weekly budget, the amount for the Long-Term Goal will be calculated as follows:

$$\$1,000 / 12 \text{ months} = \$83.33 \text{ per month}$$

Short-term goals are treated the same way—you divide the amount by the number of weeks or months in which you hope to gather enough money to buy the item.

The way to use this worksheet is to do the following:

1. Monthly or weekly budget—you decide. We recommend that you list weekly expenses.

2. Fill out the expense section of the table.

3. Sum up all the expenses and the total becomes the total amount you spend each period.

4. If you don't receive an allowance from your parents, show them your expenses and ask them if they can afford to give you money each week (or month) to cover them. Ask for suggestions on what to drop from your expense list if they can't afford to give you the money you need. If your expenses are reasonable, and they can afford it, you may find that they will give you the sum your request.

5. If you are getting an allowance, ask them to adjust it based on your "Savings and Investments" category. You may want to tell them that you'd like to buy a share of stock (that costs between

$30 and $50) every month or two after you read the rest of this book.

6. Using the numbers you filled in on Worksheet 1.1, ask your parents to let your relatives know that, as a Teenvestor, you are ready to accept cash gifts for investing in stocks or mutual funds.

7. If you are old enough to work (in some areas that means you are 16 years old or more), ask your parents to allow you to work so that you can earn income that will cover your expenses, and for savings and investments. We will discuss this later in the chapter.

8. If you have any special skills or hobbies, see if you can use them to make money by starting your own business. We will discuss this further.

9. If all else fails, and you can't get your parents to give you the allowance to cover your expenses (including your savings and investments), don't panic. Keep reading the book and you will dazzle them enough by what you know about investing in stocks that they will eventually give in (if they can afford to do so).

Convincing Your Parents You Are Responsible With Money

Most parents who can afford to don't mind giving their children an allowance as long as they know that the money will be used in a responsible way. The best thing you can do is to help your parents build trust in you. You have taken the first step already by learning how to create a budget. The other way you can get your parents to trust your judgment when it comes to handling money is to ask them to give you more responsibility to make purchases on your own. Not just to buy small items, but also to buy the more expensive things you need, on your own. Here is one example of how one young person did this in order to get her parents to trust her with more with money. At the beginning of summer, this girl asked her parents to give her some of the money that she knew they would have to spend on her school clothes for the next school year. She put that money in her savings account, and at the end of the summer she produced the money and went shopping with her parents. This may seem like no big deal to you but think about what this budding Teenvestor actually accomplished. By asking her parents for the money, she has shown that she cares that they know that she can be trusted not to spend the money on stupid stuff. By bringing it out for the shopping trip, she has proven that she can indeed be responsible with her parents' money.

Asking to hold onto some of the money that your parents intend to use to make purchases for you is always a good way to build their trust in you when it comes to handling money. But remember that the first time you misuse that money you ruin your chances of getting a reasonable allowance or getting money to invest in stocks and mutual funds.

WORKING FOR MONEY AT HOME

Besides asking for an allowance, another way to get money is to work for it. You can work around the house by doing extra chores for your parents. Please understand that we are not talking about chores you should be doing anyway such as keeping your room clean or vacuuming the living room floor. We are referring to tasks that are above what your parents expect you to do for the family. For example, if your parents expect you to mow the lawn every two weeks during the summer, you shouldn't consider that an extra chore for which you should ask for money. On the other hand, cleaning out your garage or painting some rooms in your house may be chores for which your parents will gladly pay.

You can start off by giving your parents suggestions about things you can do (besides your regular chores) to help them around the house for pay. These things should be more than little items such as running errands. They should be meaningful things and they should be tasks that require real, but safe work. Don't bother volunteering for things you are too young to do or things for which you have no real experience. For example, unless you are at least 14 years old, don't ask to paint the exterior of your house—you are too young to climb ladders and your hands may not be strong enough to properly complete the job.

GETTING A REAL JOB

Even if you are lucky enough to get an allowance from your parents or you are able to get money for doing chores around the house, there will come a time when you will want to make your own money—enough to invest in stocks and mutual funds, and enough to meet some of your long-term and short-term goals.

While this is not a book on how to get a job, there are a few things you need to know about finding employment. For one thing, don't think about working unless you are 16 years old or more. Secondly, if you are thinking about a job, you need a resume. A professional-looking resume will set you apart from the rest of your peers for any job you try out for. See our website, www.teenvestor.com, for more information on resume writing.

At your age, you may be able to get a job at fast food restaurants like McDonald's or Burger King. However, we recommend that you seek work that rewards you for how much effort you put forth. In any case, whatever job you get, remember that when you get your first pay check, "pay yourself first" by saving or investing some money. Make this a priority, otherwise the money you get will be quickly wasted.

STARTING YOUR OWN BUSINESS

Teenvestors have come a long way from running lemonade stands. These days, you are likely to find young entrepreneurs running real businesses such as building websites, selling and trading valuable baseball cards, selling T-shirts, selling hand-made dolls, and other businesses related to their hobbies and interests. Because this book does not focus on teaching you how to become an entrepreneur, we would like to point you to another book that will help: *The Lemonade Stand: A Guide To Encouraging The Entrepreneur In Your Child* by Emmanuel Modu (the co-author of this book). The book can be purchased through our website, www.teenvestor.com.

One of the benefits of starting your own business is that it can help provide you with the money you need to start investing in stocks and mutual funds. But, of course, you need a good business idea before you can even make a penny. Our website, www.teenvestor.com, has a special section for young entrepreneurs.

OPENING AN ACCOUNT

Before you can begin saving money, you need to have a place to put your money. You can stash your money in your house but if you do so, you will be tempted to use it. The best solution is to put your money in a bank.

When we were young, we could get what was called a Passbook Account that was stamped each time we deposited money. These days, a lot of banks have eliminated Passbook Accounts for young people and even charge customers with small balances a fee for maintaining their accounts. You may have to try several banks in your area to find one that will waive these fees. Quite often, you may have to open a joint account with your parents in order to avoid such a fee. The Young Americans Bank in Denver is one bank that allows Teenvestors from all over the country to open savings and checking accounts with no fee.

Our website, www.teenvestor.com will provide you with more information on saving, budgeting, starting a business, and creating a resume.

2

HELPING TEENVESTORS
MANAGE MONEY
(FOR PARENTS)

Parents go to great lengths to make sure their children receive the best education that money can buy. They send their children to music lessons, ballet lessons, tennis lessons, computer summer camps, and other skill-intensive programs and activities. Unfortunately, they neglect one of the most inexpensive and valuable skills their children can acquire—how to handle money. In a capitalist system, as we have here in the United States, knowing how to manage the money one earns is of utmost importance.

According to the Rand Youth Poll, only 35% of parents talk to their children about money. This means that the other 65% miss their best opportunity to teach their children how to budget and spend money wisely.

Sometimes parents neglect to teach their children about money because they were brought up in families that kept financial matters secret or discouraged their children's participation in decisions involving money. Parents raised in such environments are in turn applying the same flawed principles to raising their own children.

Learning the basics of how to handle money is the first step in your children's financial education. Early financial literacy will arm your Teenvestors with the knowledge they need to start investing in the stock market, mutual funds, and in other financial assets.

While not many Teenvestors will earn a great sum of money by investing, most will still have to know how to collect money, budget it, and invest it.

The best time for young people to acquire money management skills is long before they even start investing in any financial instrument. Parents must shoulder the responsibility for ensuring that their children learn the basics of handling money in these early years. By their teen years, young people should already demonstrate the financial savvy necessary to invest in the stock market.

TEACHING MONEY MANAGEMENT

There are three common approaches parents take to help their children become financially literate: giving their children money on an as–needed basis, paying their children for doing chores, and giving their children regular allowances.

Giving Money On An As-Needed Basis

Giving children money as the need arises is one approach that all parents have taken at one time or another. For example, if your daughter wants to go to the movies with her friends and she asks you for the cash, you give her the exact sum she needs. For some purchases made by your child, giving out money this way is probably okay. Unless you trust your Teenvestor's spending habits, you wouldn't want to give her money too far in advance of purchasing big-ticket items like school clothes or a computer. The one drawback to giving money on an as-needed basis is that it doesn't help your Teenvestor learn how to budget her money or make decisions about how to use that money in the future.

Tying Allowances To Chores

Another approach some parents take in introducing their children to money management is to tie allowances to specific chores. A survey taken by Penny Power, a Consumer Reports publication for young people, revealed that 90% of the children who get allowances say that they are supposed to do some work around the house for it. For example, parents might assign a dollar value to taking out the garbage, mowing the lawn, vacuuming the house, and other ordinary chores that young people would normally do (without compensation) as a member of a family. Using this approach, parents frequently also dock their children money for neglecting to do such chores.

Unfortunately, with this approach, children learn neither responsibility nor money management skills. Instead, they learn to expect payment for things that they should be doing for free, such as cleaning their rooms, setting the dinner table, or refraining from beating on their brothers and sisters. If parents tie allowances to ordinary chores, they run the risk that their children may decide (on the days they are feeling particularly lazy) to forgo their allowances by refraining from doing the chores. Parents should not mix the lessons children should learn at home about being responsible family members with lessons on how to handle money.

Giving Out Regular Allowances In Advance

The third (and the best) approach parents employ in teaching their children how to manage money is to give a regular allowance. The Teen Poll commissioned by Merrill Lynch & Co. found that 38% of teenagers receive allowance. As you will see later in this chapter, an allowance must have a component that Teenvestors can spend any way they see fit (within general parameters you have set about purchases) with little or no strings attached. However, an allowance can also include amounts that have been earmarked for specific expenditures, for savings, and for investments. The maturity of each Teenvestor will determine what portion of the allowance can be made up of money she can spend any way she sees fit and what portion is earmarked for specific purposes.

In the next section, we have outlined what we call "allowance levels" based on your Teenvestor's maturity and the level of responsibility you feel she can handle. But before you move on to this section, we want to point out the two biggest mistakes parents make in setting allowances for their children: setting allowances based on what other children in the neighborhood get from their parents and setting allowances based on what they themselves got from their parents when they were young.

Parents who set allowances according to the amounts given by other parents relinquish their right to determine the money that is appropriate for their children. In addition, these parents may find that they can't afford to dispense the same amount of money to their children as the neighbors give to theirs.

Your own childhood allowances would probably be laughable in today's economic environment. Keep this in mind: inflation over a 20-year-period can triple or quadruple prices for recreational activities. Even a movie ticket can now cost $9.50 in some areas of the country. This is probably at least three times the price of a movie ticket when you were a teenager.

A prudent way to set an allowance is to take a survey of the recreational activities for which your Teenvestor may need money and reasonable expenses for items necessary for well-being and growth. We describe how to do this in the next section.

THE FOUR ALLOWANCE LEVELS

There are four allowance levels you can dispense to your Teenvestor. Each level reflects increasingly more financial responsibility to help you gradually teach her how to handle money.

The Level 1 Allowance

The *Level 1 Allowance* is the allowance that we feel is the basic amount any Teenvestor should receive regardless of how much she knows about managing her money. It is the basis for teaching a Teenvestor how to take on more responsibility in managing and investing her money.

Worksheet 2.1, shown on the next page, is a budget worksheet that we provided your Teenvestor in the previous chapter. We will explain some of the components of the budget as we proceed to lay out the four levels of allowances.

<u>**Worksheet 2.1**</u>
Weekly Budget Example For Teenvestors

Income
1. Money From Parents $
2. Money From Relatives $
3. Money From A Job $
4. Money From A Business $

   <u>**TOTAL INCOME**</u>   <u>$ </u>

Expenses
1. School Lunch $
2. Other School Items $

3. Savings & Investments $

4. Daily Newspaper $
5. Gas(if you drive) $
6. Magazine Subscriptions $
7. Snacks $

8. Long-Term Goal $
9. Short-Term Goal $
10. Other Item #1 $
11. Other Item #2 $
12. Other Item #3 $
13. Other Item #4 $
14. Other Item #5 $

   <u>**TOTAL EXPENSES**</u>   <u>$ </u>

A reasonable Level 1 Allowance would consist of money for *discretionary expenses*. Discretionary expenses are expenses that are for recreational activities, or activities that can easily be eliminated from a budget without severely affecting your quality of life. For example, in your family's budget, a discretionary expense could be the yearly family vacation. Your children may be disappointed if you eliminate the vacation, but if money gets tight you can abandon the vacation without any long-term consequences. For Teenvestors, examples of discretionary expenses could be the cost of buying magazines from newsstands or buying electronic games. In general, discretionary expenses for your Teenvestors should consist of small amounts for leisure activities or hobbies such as going to the movies, skating rink, and video game arcade. If you normally give them money for these activities when they need it, why not bundle the money and give it to them once a week, once every two weeks, or even once a month?

Of all the allowance levels mentioned in this section, the Level 1 Allowance is the only allowance amount that should not be taken away from your Teenvestor. Whether she does her chores or not, she should continue to receive the basic allowance amount for discretionary spending as long as she continues to follow the basic moral and ethical codes you have set for the use of those funds. We want to emphasize that because this amount is discretionary, you should not tell her exactly how to spend it.

The Level 2 Allowance

The next level of allowance that you can give your Teenvestor, if she has demonstrated that she can handle the Level 1 Allowance, is the *Level 2 Allowance*. The Level 2 Allowance is the Level 1 Allowance plus some *nondiscretionary items*. Nondiscretionary items are expenses that must be paid, no matter what. In your family's budget, the nondiscretionary items could be your rent or mortgage.

When you first move from giving your Teenvestor the Level 1 Allowance to the Level 2 Allowance, you should include only small nondiscretionary items. Such nondiscretionary items could be school lunch money (which should now be given in one lump sum), bus money and other small expenditures that may contribute to her growth and well-being.

Later, as you begin to trust her spending habits, you can add money for other nondiscretionary items, such as shoes and clothing, to her allowance. It could take a few months or a year before you can give her more responsibility for her nondiscretionary expenditures—it simply depends on your Teenvestor's maturity.

Once again, how much money you dispense in the *Level 2 Allowance* depends on your own personal financial situation. The Level 2 Allowance can be taken away if your Teenvestor is not meeting your expectation on how she should spend the amount. When you yank her Level 2 Allowance privileges, go back to giving her the Level 1 Allowance amount.

It is possible that some Teenvestors will not be excited about getting money in their allowances for nondiscretionary expenditures since, by definition, they have no choice as to how that money is to be spent. In other words, the money is already earmarked for specific expenses. Most Teenvestors, however, will appreciate the fact that they have been entrusted with more responsibility in terms of more money to use for their needs. Yes, even the illusion of more wealth can help Teenvestors learn about managing that wealth.

Another thing that can make receiving nondiscretionary money more palatable for Teenvestors is that they can't move to the *Level 3 Allowance,* which includes money for their savings accounts and for investments, without first satisfying the Level 2 Allowance requirements.

The Level 3 Allowance

The *Level 3 Allowance* is the Level 2 Allowance plus a savings and investments component of the budget on Worksheet 2.1 (expense line number 3). The "Savings & Investments" line is the amount of money your Teenvestor should put in a bank or invest in stocks, mutual funds, or other financial assets. It is important to note that in this category savings really means money that is not earmarked for particular expenditures. It is money put away for emergencies. Investments represent money put into (or earmarked for) financial assets in hopes of making some interest or profit.

Budgeting experts consider the amount set aside for savings and investing as an integral part of a budget. It is so important that some call the act of setting aside money in this category "paying yourself first." By "paying yourself first" they mean that once you have paid the bills that are necessary for your survival, the next thing to do is to put money aside for savings and investments. Nothing else should take a higher priority. We mentioned this concept to your Teenvestor in the previous chapter but we think that you must emphasize its importance when she approaches you for an allowance.

There are steps you can take to encourage your Teenvestor to save and invest money in stocks or other financial instruments.

The first thing you can do, of course, is to give her money specifically to put in her bank account (if it is practical to establish an account) for emergency purposes or in anticipation of making investments. This, as we stated earlier, moves the Level 2 Allowance to a Level 3 Allowance.

Another thing you can very easily do is to set up your own money-matching program for any additional amount she puts aside in her bank account for investing. For example, if she would ordinarily put aside an additional $10 each week for savings and investments, you can add another $10 to it as long as that money will be truly used for its intended purpose.

Saving and investing are good habits to establish in your Teenvestor. Even if she does not understand the value of saving and investing, make her put the money in this category in the bank anyway (or put it in your own bank account on her behalf).

Because savings and investments are such important components of the allowance (and hence, the budget), you will have to periodically monitor the amount saved and invested to see if your Teenvestor is accumulating the amounts she should. Obviously, a bank account is a necessary part of this process and you should help her open one unless she can piggy-back on your account.

The Level 3 Allowance privileges should be taken away if your Teenvestor is not meeting your expectations on how she should spend the nondiscretionary portion of the allowance. When you take away her Level 3 Allowance privileges, go back to the Level 2 Allowance amount.

The Level 4 Allowance

The *Level 4 Allowance* is the Level 3 Allowance plus "Long-Term Goal" and "Short-Term Goal" components.

Most young people seek instant pleasure. From the time they are born to the time they go off to college, most children want immediate gratification. When they are old enough to understand the concept of money, they easily settle into a compulsive buying mentality unless their parents have taught them good money management skills.

One of the biggest challenges you will face is getting your Teenvestor to plan for expenditures. An important step in helping your children develop a money management plan is to have them set their own *goals*.

Goals are wants, needs and future objectives your Teenvestor can set for herself. In the context of teaching Teenvestors how to manage their money, financial goals are the amount of money put aside for specific purchases.

These goals may be long-term or short-term in nature. While you may consider long-term goals to be objectives you hope to reach in five to ten years, teens have much shorter time frames. For a 14-year-old Teenvestor, a long-term goal could have a time horizon of one year and a short-term goal could have a time horizon of a month.

Two important expense categories necessary for determining allowance for your Teenvestors are "Long-Term Goals" (expense item 8) and "Short-Term Goals" (expense item 9) on Worksheet 2.1.

In the previous chapter, we advised Teenvestors to include short-term and long-term goals in their budgets. They can do so by spreading the expenses of the items they want to buy over the period of time in which they hope to have sufficient amount of money set aside for the purchase. For example, if your Teenvestor wants to buy a $1,000 computer in a year, she has to spread the cost over a 52-week period like so:

$1,000 / 52 weeks = $19.23 per week
or
$1,000 / 12 months = $83.33 per month (if the budget is created monthly)

We consider this a long-term goal because it will take a year for your Teenvestor to save the amount of money she needs to make the purchase. This means that on the expense side of a weekly budget, she would have to include a figure of $19.23 in the Long-Term Goals line.

Likewise, short-term purchasing goals should also be spread out over the period of time in which the expenditure will be made. To buy a $50 item over the next two months, for example, your Teenvestor will have to spread her expenses over an 8-week period:

$50 / 8 weeks = $6.25 per week (for weekly budgets)
or
$50 / 2 months = $25 per month (for monthly budgets)

So, on the expense side of the budget (expense item 9), your Teenvestor should enter $6.25 if she creates a weekly budget or $25 if she creates a monthly budget.

The amounts for the long-term and short-term goals should be placed in a bank account and you should be watching their accumulation.

As is the case with other allowance levels, the Level 4 Allowance should be taken away if your Teenvestor is not meeting your expectation on how she should spend the money. When you cancel her Level 4 Allowance privileges, go back to the Level 3 or Level 2 Allowance levels.

SOURCES OF INCOME FOR YOUR TEENVESTORS

The allowance you have decided to give your Teenvestor is only one source of income in her budget. On Worksheet 2.1, the allowance to Teenvestors is listed as "Money From Parents" (income item 1). Depending on the age of your Teenvestor, you should not feel any obligation to be the sole provider of income. Remember that as long as you have decided on what expense items you will pay for, it is up to your Teenvestor to come up with other ways to take care of the other expenses in her budget unless she is simply too young to come up with other income on her own. In this section, we will discuss the various other sources of money for your Teenvestor.

Money and Other Gifts From Relatives

Teenvestors receive money from grandparents, aunts and uncles for birthdays, Christmas, Easter, Bar Mitzvahs, and other special occasions. You may want to have these relatives give you the money for disbursement to your Teenvestor if you feel that she is not responsible enough to spend the money wisely. One solution is to advise these relatives to earmark some of the funds for investing in stocks, mutual funds and other financial assets.

Relatives (including parents) can help Teenvestors start investment portfolios by giving them assets other than cash. They can give gifts such as stocks, mutual funds, bonds and other assets. These gifts can be given without adverse tax consequences for the relatives, the parents, and the Teenvestors who are the beneficiaries of the gifts. Under current tax laws, gifts of less than $10,000 each year are not subject to a gift tax and thus, neither the gift givers nor the recipients are required to pay taxes on the gifts. This is known as the "gift tax exclusion." The only condition that must be met is that the recipients of the gifts must have what's called a "present interest" in the gifts. That is, the gifts must be wholly and completely available to the recepients as soon as the gifts are actually given. Please consult a tax guide for more details on gifts.

Working Inside The Home

The other source of income for your Teenvestor, to fill in the gap in her budget, is money from doing extra chores around the house. Please understand that we are not talking about chores your Teenvestor should be doing anyway, such as keeping her room clean or vacuuming your living room floor. We are referring to tasks that are above and beyond your expectations of what she should be doing as a member of the family. If, for example, you expect your Teenvestor to put dirty dishes into the dishwasher every day, she should not ask you for compensation. On the other hand, it probably makes sense to pay your Teenvestor for cleaning out your garage or painting rooms in your house—difficult tasks that go beyond the mundane family chores.

Working Outside Of The Home

At some point, your Teenvestor will need more money for more discretionary expenditures. The allowance you give her, the amount of money you pay her for extra chores and the amount of money from relatives will eventually cease to be sufficient. She will simply need more income to meet her needs.

One way for your Teenvestor to fill this financial gap is to get a job. According to the Teen Poll commissioned by Merrill Lynch & Co., 22% of teenagers work. We feel it's a good idea for any Teenvestor 16 years old or older to seek employment. Most Teenvestors may come to that conclusion on their own anyway because at some point, when they want more things and more discretionary money, their parents will not be able to meet their financial needs. We firmly believe, however, that the criteria for allowing your Teenvestor to work outside of the house should be that:

1. Her expenditures meet the standards you have set as far as what is acceptable in your eyes.

2. She continues a certain level of savings and investments (that is, she must continue to "pay herself first.")

3. She continues to draft up her weekly or monthly budget.

4. The job does not interfere with her schoolwork.

HOW TO SET THE ALLOWANCE PERIOD

The period between each allowance can vary according to how your Teenvestor handles her money. Some 13-year olds who are given an allowance on a monthly basis can make their allowances last until the end of the month but others may spend it all in a week or a day. For children less than 13 years old, it is probably advisable to give weekly allowances. For older children, it depends on their maturity. If your Teenvestor cannot properly manage her money within the allowance time frame upon which you have decided, shorten the period between allowances.

According to child-care experts, parents should dispense allowances at designated dates and times. This gives children the opportunity to plan the activities for which they will use the discretionary portions of their allowances. Since you want your Teenvestor to learn how to properly budget for expenditures, you should not change the period between allowances without telling her in advance. In addition, you should never withhold allowance because she has been mischievous or has neglected to perform certain tasks.

THE ONGOING MONITORING OF ALLOWANCES

No allowance figure should be set in stone. You can (and should) change the allowance depending on how well your Teenvestor is handling the responsibility she has been given. The allowance can also change based on your own financial situation. If you lose your job, you may have to reduce or even eliminate the discretionary amount you are giving your Teenvestor.

One clear way of monitoring how your Teenvestor is handling the amount she is getting is to watch how she is handling her bank or investment account. If you are giving her money that she has promised to save or invest, you should see the savings accumulating in her savings or investment accounts.

Remember that if she is not spending money as she has outlined in her budget, you can pull away some of the allowance privileges except for the discretionary amount in the Level 1 Allowance.

Our website, www.teenvestor.com, will give you more information about teaching your children how to manage money.

3

INVESTMENT BASICS

We find that the best way to teach Teenvestors about stocks is to take them through the basics of a small business. Believe it or not, the most important concepts in investing in stocks can be illustrated even with a business as simple as a lemonade stand. In our camp, Teen Business Camp, we teach stock market basics by using businesses teenagers can relate to such as a T-shirt business, a gift-basket business, or even a limousine service to illustrate all the important items to look for when evaluating the stock of a company.

In this chapter, we will use a T-shirt business to illustrate basic ideas behind stock ownership. After reading this chapter, a budding Teenvestor like you will begin to see that getting stock smart can be exciting and fun.

RAISING MONEY

Susan and four other partners have decided to start their own T-shirt business, SportsTee. Her high school of 3,000 students has some of the best sports programs in the country, and her community is very supportive of high school athletics. Susan and her friends are confident that a T-shirt business will thrive in such a sports-oriented community. SportsTee will sell high quality T-shirts, painted with sports themes, at high school sporting events.

Susan and her SportsTee partners come up with a rough estimate of the amount of money they would need in order to start the business. They do this by figuring out how much the equipment will cost them, how many shirts they will have to purchase initially, and how much cash they will need on hand to meet initial expenses such as salary and rent, in order to keep the business running for a two-month period before they actually start making any money.

This method is very similar to the way that many companies determine how much money to raise by issuing stock or borrowing money. They usually figure out what they want to do—whether to start a business, to expand an existing business, or to buy new equipment to improve the business. The companies then go about issuing stock or borrowing money in order to finance these activities.

Since Susan and her friends are just starting SportsTee, their first concern is to raise enough money to buy the company's initial inventory of shirts to sell, to purchase equipment such as buckets and paints, to pay the salaries of their helpers, and to advertise the business. As you can see from the list of expenses identified on Table 3.1, Susan and her partners calculate that an initial investment of $3,500 is needed to get SportsTee off the ground.

TABLE 3.1
SportsTee's Initial Start-Up Costs
(For Two Months Of Operation)

1.	Cost Or Raw (Unpainted) Shirts	$600
2.	Cost Of Paint For Initial Purchase Of Shirts	$400
3.	Brushes	$100
4.	Bucket (Highest Quality)	$120
5.	Rental Of Space Per Year	$200
6.	Overalls For Painting	$150
7.	Advertising	$500
8.	Total Labor By All 5 Owners	$1,200
9.	Miscellaneous	$230
	Total Initial Cash Start-Up Costs	**$3,500**

For Susan and her four partners, the next task is to figure out how to raise the $3,500 they need to start SportsTee. They can raise the money by using any one of the following methods:

1. First, Susan and her partners can invest their own $3,500 to start the company.

2. Second, SportsTee can borrow the money and pay interest to the people from whom they borrow the money. Susan and her partners would still be the owners of the company except that if they don't pay the loan back they can lose the company to the lenders.

3. Third, Susan and her partners can decide to let other investors (besides the five who started the company) put money into Sports-Tee to help get it going.

THE DIFFERENCE BETWEEN EQUITY AND DEBT

Susan and her four partners decide that they will each contribute $500 of their own money, making a total partner contribution of $2,500 ($500 from each of the five partners). This $2,500 figure is called *equity*. In any business, equity is the amount of money the owners contribute to a business.

All five owners of SportsTee also decide to take out a $1,000 loan by borrowing $200 from the parents of each partner. Not surprisingly, the parents don't turn over the cash without tying a few conditions to the loan. They agree to lend SportsTee the $1,000 on the condition that (1) the loan will be repaid at an interest rate of 10% per year, (2) $600 of the borrowed funds will be repaid within one year, and (3) the other $400 will be repaid in two years. In addition, the parents warn that if SportsTee does not repay the loan in this way, the parents will either (1) take over the business or (2) if the parents feel that the business won't make it, they will stop giving out allowances until the money is paid back.

The $1,000 that SportsTee borrows is called debt. Debt is sometimes referred to as *short-term debt* or *long-term debt* depending upon the length of the repayment period. Debt is referred to as short-term debt if it is to be repaid within a year. Debt is referred to as long-term debt if it is to be repaid in over one year. Applying this rule of thumb to the borrowing, SportsTee's short-term debt is $600 while its long-term debt is $400. Furthermore, debt can be *secured* or *unsecured*. SportsTee debt is secured because its lenders can go after whatever the company owns if the company does not pay its debts on time. Remember that Susan and her partners agree that if they fail to pay back the loan they will either (1) have to turn over the business to their parents or (2) they each will have to forgo their allowances until the money is paid back. The debt would be considered unsecured if the parents have no right to go after what the Teenvestors own if the loans are not paid back at the specified time.

Between the $2,500 in equity that Susan and her partners come up with from their own bank accounts and the $1,000 that they borrow from their parents, the SportsTee partners collect $3,500 to get their T-shirt business started. This combined total of equity and debt is commonly referred to as *capital*.

Public and Private Companies

Susan and her four partners are the sole owners of SportsTee. For this reason, it is called a *private* company because only Susan and her four partners (and whomever else they want to invite) are allowed to invest in the company and make decisions about the direction of the company. Unlike SportsTee, many established companies are called *public* companies because ownership of these companies is open to the general public—anybody can invest in the company. In a public company, pieces of the company, commonly known as *shares*, are owned by *shareholders* (also known as equity holders) or investors. One of the biggest reasons companies decide to *go public* (to offer shares of the company to the public) is that public companies can raise capital more easily. When public companies need money, they can sell investors shares in their businesses in return for cash.

Now this is where you, as a Teenvestor, would enter the picture. In public companies, equity is usually made up of *common stock*, *preferred stock*, and *retained earnings*.

Common stockholders not only own a piece of the company but they also vote for the *board of directors* (the people who are responsible for overseeing the company). This means that common stockholders control the management of the company. Whether or not these investors profit from their investment depends upon how well the company performs. Common stockholders receive *dividends*—a portion of a company's profit that is distributed to stockholders.

Preferred stockholders receive dividends but these dividends are based on a specific dollar amount of principal (similar to interest payments on loans). Preferred stockholders get paid before common stockholders get a piece of a company's profit. However, unlike common stockholders, preferred stockholders can't vote to elect the board of directors.

As you will learn later in this book, a company can do three things with the money it makes: it can distribute all its profits to its shareholders, it can keep all the money to expand the business, or it can distribute part of the money to shareholders and keep part of it to grow the company. Retained earnings are the company's profit that's put back into the company to help expand it so that it can make more money in the future.

RISK IN BUSINESS

When a company goes out of business, the people to whom the company owes money get paid before the equity holders. So for SportsTee, the partners' parents who loaned the company $1,000 get their money back first after the company sells off everything it owns such as the buckets and the brushes if it goes broke. Any money left over goes to Susan and her four partners. So, as you can see, a lender's advantage is that she is first in line to recover a loan when things go wrong. A lender's disadvantage, on the other hand, is that she can't make more money even if the company does phenomenally well. For example, the parents who lend SportsTee money are entitled only to interest payments on their money. The investors in the business (stockholders or equity holders) are entitled to any profit the company makes (if the company decides to distribute all the profits to its stockholders). The problem for the SportsTee partners, though, is that there is no guarantee the company will make money, so they are taking a lot more *risk*. When we talk about risk in a business, we are talking about how likely it is to lose money in that business. The greater the chance of loosing money, the higher the risk. In general, stocks are riskier than loans.

INITIAL PUBLIC OFFERINGS

Sometimes a company starts out as a private company and later becomes a public company. In general, when a private company wants to raise capital and issue stock to the public for the first time, the company sells stock through an *Initial Public Offering* or *IPO*. This process, commonly referred to as "going public," typically involves the following:

1. The company hires *underwriters* investment bankers who agree to help with the IPO. The bankers can do one of two things. They can buy up all the shares the company wants to offer and then resell these shares to the public at a slightly higher price, keeping the profit. Alternatively, instead of buying up the shares from the company and then reselling

63

them to investors, the bankers can just find buyers for the shares for a fee.

2. The underwriters and the company put together a *prospectus*—a document that maps out the nature of the business of the company making the IPO, its financial history, its management team, and other important information for potential investors.

3. The underwriters offer the shares to the public by putting an advertisement, called a *tombstone*, in publications.

4. The underwriters go on a visit, also known as a *road show*, with potential buyers to convince them that the stock is worth buying.

To illustrate the IPO process, let's go back to SportsTee. Assume that Susan and her partners find that the T-shirt business is a terrific idea and SportsTee is a phenomenal success. The SportsTee partners now want to expand the business to operate in other schools. Besides, Susan's parents have said that SportsTee may no longer operate in the basement of their house—the partners are making too much noise at all hours of the night, they're leaving junk all over the house and the household grocery bill has almost doubled since SportsTee began its operation. Under these conditions, SportsTee decides to go public in order to raise more capital to expand its business in a larger space.

Susan approaches her friend Andy, who has lots of money and is experienced at helping companies raise money. After analyzing the situation, Andy tells Susan that he can help her go public.

Susan and Andy figure that SportsTee needs an additional $4,000 to meet its capital needs. They reach this figure by considering a number of factors, including: how much SportsTee would make each year if it were to expand, who would be running the company, how much it would cost to relocate, and the competition the company will face in the future.

After analyzing the situation, Andy determines that SportsTee can find 40 Teenvestors willing to invest $100 in SportsTee for a total of $4,000. He intends to help SportsTee sell the 40 shares of stock to other investors and keep a small commission of 7% ($7 for every $100 of stock he sells) for his efforts.

In order to find investors who will buy the shares, Andy needs to make up a brochure to describe SportsTee, outline its financial projections and tell how terrific the SportsTee idea is. In addition, Andy has to place an ad in the local and high school newspapers in order to get 40 investors.

Once Andy finds the 40 investors, sells the SportsTee shares to them and makes his $280 in commissions, he is out of the picture—he will no longer be involved in any transactions between SportsTee and its 40 investors.

What we have just illustrated is a very simplified version of an IPO. While it may be simple, we have covered some of the components of a real IPO. In the example, Andy plays the role of the underwriter, the brochure he creates is like the prospectus, and the advertisement he puts in the paper is the same as a tombstone in a real IPO. The only things that are missing here are the legal papers that have to be filed as required by the Securities and Exchange Commission, a government agency.

Recall that SportsTee has five original investors (Susan and her friends). With the 40 additional investors, it now has 45 investors in total. In real life, an IPO involves much larger companies with millions of shares offered to the public in what is referred to as a *primary market*. A primary market is the activity when shares are sold directly to the public for the first time. Once the public purchases all of these shares, anyone who wants a share will have to buy it from someone else who has bought one. These shares are sold in what is called the *secondary market*. The secondary market occurs when shares are bought from others or sold to others through people known as *brokers* who work in *stock exchanges*—places where the trading of stock is actually done.

The concept of a primary market and secondary market is important enough to go over in more detail with an example. The only time a company issuing stock benefits from that issuance is in the primary market—that is, when investors buy new shares issued in an IPO and give money over to that company. When an investor buys stock from another investor (which is the case nearly all the time), the company that initially issued the stock does not get any more money from any investor. A good example would be if your parents bought a new car from General Motors (GM). At the time of their purchase, GM gets the money for the car and that money helps increase its profits. But suppose your parents then sell the car a few years later to a neighbor. GM is no longer in the picture so the company will not get a piece of the money your parents get for selling their used car. In this example, buying a brand new car is much like buying shares issued in an IPO in the primary market. Selling the car a few years later is like selling shares in the secondary market.

There are a few major exchanges where brokers actually buy and sell shares of public companies in the secondary market for their clients: the New York Stock Exchange, the NASDAQ, and the American Stock Exchange. We will discuss these exchanges further in Chapter 8.

ASSIGNMENT 3.1

The Best Answers To The Following Questions.

If you own this type of stock, you can help determine the members of the board of directors of the company in which you have invested.
1.   Preferred Stock
2.   Long-Term Debt
3.   Common Stock
4.   Assets

Assume you started your own company by borrowing money from your parents and also investing some of your own money. Which item below represents the total amount of money you put into your company to get it started?
1.   Capital
2.   Equity
3.   Long-Term Debt
4.   Common Stock

A document that shows exactly what a company owns or owes.
1.   Prospectus
2.   Balance Sheet
3.   IPO
4.   Tombstone

(Cont'd On Next Page)

ASSIGNMENT 3.1 CONT'D

Please Choose The Best Answers To The Following Questions.

An Underwriter is:
1. an individual or company that helps a company with an IPO
2. an individual who owns common stock
3. an individual or company that lends or borrows money
4. an individual who owns preferred stock

Our website, www.teenvestor.com, will give you more information about debt, capital, equity, dividends, risk, IPOs, and other relevant topics.

4

BALANCE SHEET BASICS

If a stranger asked you to invest in his business, the first question you should ask yourself is this: how do I know that I will get my money back? To answer this question, you would want to know the type of business this individual runs, what equipment his company owns in order to make his product or deliver his service, the amount of money he has borrowed from other people, and the amount of money from his own bank account he has already invested in the business. The answer to all these questions will give you a more comfortable feeling about parting with your hard-earned money. A *balance sheet* will give you some of the answers to these questions.

THE PIECES OF A BALANCE SHEET

A balance sheet is a snapshot of what a company owns (or assets), what it owes (or *liabilities*), and the amount of money the owners have invested in the company (or *shareholder's equity* or *owner's equity* or just plain *equity*). One thing that is always true about balance sheets is that assets are equal to the sum of liabilities and share-holder's equity. In other words, the formula below must always hold true:

Assets = Liabilities + Equity

This always holds true because what a company owns (its assets) are purchased by the money the company either borrowed (liabilities) or has acquired through the contributions of the partners (shareholder's equity).

The balance sheet is produced based on an idea developed more than 500 years ago called "double-entry accounting" by an Italian mathematician named Luca Pacioli. Double-entry accounting provides an easy way for businesses to keep track of their assets, liabilities, and shareholder's equity.

To illustrate how such a system works, let's use the SportsTee example from the previous chapter. Recall that initially the company collected $3,500 in cash because the 5 partners each contributed $500 of their own money and also borrowed a total of $1,000 from their parents. If SportsTee uses $680 of that money to buy equipment, it has to record (on paper or in a computer spreadsheet) the transaction this way:

Cash went down by $680 ($2,820 remains in bank)
The value of equipment went up by $680

As you can see, the business can trace exactly what happened to its money by showing what items increased in value and what items decreased in value. Notice that the purchase of the equipment forced SportsTee to make two entries in a book where it keeps its records. One entry shows that it pulled cash out of its bank account, and another shows that the balance of the equipment it owns went up by the same amount. This method of keeping track of a company's activity is called double-entry accounting because at least two types of *accounts* (categories of assets, liabilities, and equity) are always affected. Things can get more complicated than this but we hope you understand the basic idea.

Balance sheets have dates attached to them because assets, liabilities and shareholder's equity can change every day. So when you see a balance sheet, you will probably also see the date it was created on the top of the table.

Let's go back to our SportsTee example to understand balance sheets. Given SportsTee's initial investment, a balance sheet that shows the company's assets, liabilities and shareholder's equity can be put together.

Table 4.1, on the next page, shows SportsTee's balance sheet on its first day of operation. This balance sheet was created using the balances from Table 3.1 in the previous chapter, which shows the total amount the partners need to open up the business.

On Table 4.1, SportsTee's assets are broken down into two sections: *Current Assets* and *Property, Plant & Equipment (Fixed Assets)*. The current assets consist of: cash set aside for advertisement, cash set aside to pay workers, cash set aside for rent, money set aside for miscellaneous purchases, and the value of the inventory (i.e., raw T-shirts). The total current asset balance is $2,820.

Property, plant and equipment on the balance sheet consist of paint, brushes, buckets, and overalls. It totals $680. The total asset balance is $3,500.

TABLE 4.1
SportsTee's Initial Balance Sheet
(On Its First Day Of Operation)

Current Assets	
Cash, Inventory (Raw Shirts)	$ 2,820
Property, Plant, & Equipment (Fixed Assets)	
Brushes, Paints, Overalls, Bucket	$680
Total Assets	**$3,500**
Liabilities	
Short-Term Debt (Or Current Liabilities) &	$600
Long-Term Debt	$400
Equity (Including Retained Earnings)	$2,500
Total Liabilities + Equity	**$3,500**

SportsTee was able to buy these assets because of the $3,500 acquired by using the $2,500 contributed by the partners (the equity) and the $1,000 they borrowed (the liability). Therefore, the liability and equity balance is $3,500. When you think about it, this makes perfect sense because all assets owned by SportsTee was acquired by using the money its owners borrowed or contributed. It is worth repeating that this fundamental accounting concept can be represented by the following mathematical formula:

Assets = Liabilities (borrowed money) + Equity (contributed money)

ASSIGNMENTS 4.1 TO 4.2

Assignment 4.1: If a company's asset balance is $100,000 and its liability balance is $80,000, what is its equity?

Assignment 4.2: If a company has equity of $50,000 and liabilities of $150,000, what is the balance of its assets?

THE TYPICAL CORPORATE BALANCE SHEET

In all balance sheets, you will find the asset, liability and shareholder's equity categories. However, when you start to look at balance sheets for companies in different businesses, you will see big differences in the details of what makes up assets and liabilities. For example, the assets of a car manufacturer like Ford Motor Company will include the big equipment the company uses to make cars. But how about a company whose assets is its business know-how? For example, an accounting firm like KPMG, which provides accounting services to big corporations, will have smaller fixed assets than Ford. This is understandable because KPMG does not really manufacture anything. The company simply provides services through its employees—whether it is creating balance sheets for companies or telling companies how to run their businesses better. To bring it closer to home, suppose you started a business where you advise people in your neighborhood on the type of computer to purchase. In this case, your company's asset is you—specifically the information you will provide your customers. Unfortunately, the double-entry accounting method does not have a good way for you to record yourself and your knowledge as an asset on the balance sheet. For this reason, we will concentrate on the balance sheets of manufacturing companies to illustrate the typical corporate balance sheet. As you start getting interested in industries that offer information and business know-how, you can learn about the structure of their balance sheets. This chapter is just to give you a taste of some of the ways information is presented to you about companies and how you can use the information to help you determine if you should invest or not.

The balance sheets for most big companies that manufacture products will look a little different from SportsTee's balance sheet. For one thing, the asset, liability and equity balances for big companies are much bigger. The most recent year-end asset, liability and equity figures (rounded to the nearest million) for Ford are as follows:

Assets:	$284,421,000,000
Liabilities:	$265,811,000,000
Equity:	$18,610,000,000

Another reason why the balance sheet of most big companies will look different from SportsTee's balance sheet is that these companies have been in business for a long time, so there are categories of assets and liabilities that reflect this fact.

Table 4.2, on the next page, shows the categories in which many manufacturing companies place their assets, liabilities, and equity. The assets in this typical balance sheet are broken out into current assets and fixed assets.

TABLE 4.2
The Typical Corporate Balance Sheet Items
(For Manufacturing Companies)

Total Assets

Current Assets
      Cash
      Marketable Securities
      Accounts Receivable
      Inventory

Fixed Assets
      Property, Plant, & Equipment (at Cost)
        Less Depreciation
      Prepaid Expenses
      Patents and Goodwill

Liabilities & Equity

Total Current Liabilities
      Accounts Payable
      Notes Payable
      Accrued Expenses

Total Long-Term Liabilities
      Long-Term Debt

Equity
      Common Stock
      Preferred Stock
      Retained Earnings

Current Assets On The Corporate Balance Sheet

This balance sheet shows that the current assets are made up of: cash in bank accounts; marketable securities—certificates of deposits (CDs); U.S. Treasury Bills and Notes; and others items that can easily be converted to cash; *accounts receivable*—the amount of money owed to the company for goods sold or services delivered; and in-ventory—the value of finished goods and raw materials.

Fixed Assets On Corporate Balance Sheet

Fixed assets are made up of: property, plant, and equipment (less depreciation)—buildings, machines, and land used by the com-pany to produce the company's products (see an explanation of de-preciation later in this chapter); prepaid expenses—expenses the com-pany pays ahead of time such as rent; patents and goodwill; market-able securities—long-term certificates of deposit (CDs), long-term U.S. Treasury Bills and Notes, and other items that mature in over one year.

Current Liabilities On The Corporate Balance Sheet

On Table 4.2, the typical corporate current liabilities are broken down into three sections: accounts payable—money the company owes for products or services it has purchased; notes payable—money the company has borrowed for a short period of time (usually a year or less); accrued expenses—wages, taxes and other expenses that the company has not yet paid but should pay shortly.

Accrued Expenses is worthy of further explanation. This ex-pense item is on the balance sheet because the company will have to pay some expenses every two weeks (wages, for example), every three months (taxes, for example), or every month (rent or leases, for example), but it has to accumulate the expenses before the payment date. For example, if you pay your friend $7 each week, once a week, for a task he helps you do around the house, you will add $1 to ac-crued expenses on your personal balance sheet each day, until the seventh day when you'd have to pay him. At that time, accrued expenses go back down to zero because you have made the payment. Accrued expenses allow companies to keep track of bills like wages and other items they pay periodically.

Long-Term Liabilities On The Corporate Balance Sheet

On Table 4.2, the typical corporate long-term liability is simply the money owed by the company due in over one year. Remember that this money has been borrowed from lenders who expect to be paid interest on the loan whether the company does well or not.

Equity And Retained Earnings On The Corporate Balance Sheet

On Table 4.2, the typical corporate equity amount consists of common stock, preferred stock and retained earnings. Recall that common stock and preferred stock are the money put into the company by investors, and retained earnings are the profit kept by the company (and not distributed as dividends). Please note that unlike SportsTee, which initially had 5 investors or shareholders, a company like Ford Motor Company had 1.91 billion shares outstanding at the time of this writing.

DEPRECIATION

While it isn't necessary to go through every single category of the typical company balance sheet in greater detail at this time, there is at least one category under fixed (or long-term) assets you should be aware of: *depreciation*.

Depreciation is an important concept because it reflects how much of your assets have been used up. You may recall from the previous chapter that SportsTee had to buy a high quality bucket for $120 in order to create its product. Let's assume that the bucket will be worn out in four years so SportsTee will have to discard it at the end of the four-year period. If SportsTee expects the bucket to be worthless in 4 years, it means that each year, the company will use up 1/4th of the bucket's value or approximately $30 (1/4 x $120). At the end of the first year, for example, the value of the bucket used up would be $30 (1/4 x $120). See Table 4.3, on the next page, for an illustration of depreciation. If SportsTee had a balance sheet for the end of the year, the bucket would be shown as presented on Table 4.3 (under the column labeled "End Of Year 1"). That is, the original value of the bucket will be shown, followed by a depreciation amount (which is a negative number), and then the final value of the bucket, reflecting the depreciation.

This reduction in the value of the assets is considered an expense and it should reduce the income SportsTee reports to the Internal Revenue Service, the tax collector for the U.S. government. For simplicity, we have ignored the depreciation of the SportsTee assets on its balance.

Depreciation is important for understanding *book value*—the value of the company if it goes bankrupt. Book value will be further discussed in the next chapter. For some investors, it is an important figure to know when trying to determine whether they should invest in a company or not.

TABLE 4.3
SportsTee Depreciation Item On Balance Sheet
(Day 1 Depreciation Compared With Year-End Depreciation)

	Day 1	End Of Year 1
Bucket	$120	$120
Depreciation	-$ 0	-$ 30
Net Value	$120	$ 90

Our website, www.teenvestor.com, will give you more information about balance sheets.

5

WHAT THE BALANCE SHEET REVEALS

The balance sheet can answer three basic questions that should be on the mind of all Teenvestors when evaluating a company:

- Can the company pay its debt?
- Has the company borrowed too much money?
- What is the company worth if it goes out of business?

In the next few sections we will explain how a balance sheet can help you answer these questions.

CAN THE COMPANY PAY THOSE IT OWES MONEY?

There are some tests a beginning investor can easily perform on a company's balance sheet just to see if that company can pay its bills. The first test checks whether the company has enough money to pay back debt that is due right away. The second test checks whether the balances of specific items on the company's assets and liabilities are improving or getting worse.

Current Ratio

Whether the company can pay those it owes money, otherwise known as *creditors*, depends on how much cash it can get its hands on when the bills are due. Just think of your own personal situation at home. Whether your parents can pay the electricity or phone bill depends on whether they have cash in the bank, whether they can borrow money to pay the bill, or whether they can sell off their assets (such as a car) to gather enough cash to pay the bill.

The reality is that your parents can't really depend on selling their car as a way to pay such bills because it may take a long time to find a buyer for the car and negotiate the proper sale price. In short, their ability to pay their bills (a bill being a form of current liabilities) depends on their current assets, and not on their fixed or long-term assets because current assets consist of either cash or assets that can be easily sold off to get cash. In order to determine whether a company can pay its bills, you have to look at the size of its current assets versus its current liabilities. On the SportsTee balance sheet on Table 5.1, shown on the next page, the current asset balance is $2,820 while the current liability balance (which is short-term debt in this case) is $600. With these two numbers, we can calculate the *current ratio* by dividing the current asset by the current liabilities:

Current Ratio = Current Assets / Current Liabilities

Current Ratio = $2,820 / $600 = 4.7

TABLE 5.1
SportsTee Initial Balance Sheet
(On Its First Day Of Operation)

Current Assets

    Cash, Inventory (Raw Shirts) $2,820

Property, Plant, & Equipment

    Brushes, Paints, Overalls, Bucket $680

    Total Assets   **$3,500**

Liabilities

    Short-Term Debt (Or Current Liabilities) & $600

    Long-Term Debt $400

Equity (Includes Retained Earnings) $2,500

    Total Liabilities + Equity   **$3,500**

This ratio indicates that current assets are nearly 5 times the size of current liabilities. The way to interpret this current ratio is that SportsTee has about 5 times as much cash and other items it can quickly turn into cash to pay off bills that will soon become due. This figure makes sense only if you compare the current ratios of the same company over a period of time or if you compare the current ratio of different companies in the same type of business. The higher the current ratio, the better. A high current ratio does not guarantee that a company is a winner. It is only one of the indicators among many that can help tell you if the company is worth a second look.

Changes In Asset Balances

You will find that what really matters with a balance sheet is how it changes from year to year (or period to period). From this point of view, we will take a look at a few major items on a typical company balance sheet to see how the increase or decrease in balances helps or hurts the company.

Cash

Cash is the money the company has on hand or in bank accounts. In general, we consider an increase in cash to be a good thing because it can indicate that the company can better withstand hard times when things get difficult.

Accounts Receivable

An increase in accounts receivable is not necessarily good news. Recall that accounts receivable indicates the amount of money owed to the company by its customers. A high accounts receivable balance sounds like it might be a good thing until you discover that the company has already claimed that amount as part of its profit.

A good example would be if you sold your bicycle to an unreliable friend for $150 but you have not yet received the cash from him yet. On your personal balance sheet, you will have an account receivable entry for $150. Now, you can brag to your other friends that you sold the bike at a good price, but the fact that you have not yet received the money makes your claim questionable because you may never receive that money. Most businesses do the same thing you have done with the sale of your bike. They "brag" (by showing the $150 on a statement that indicates how much money they have made) about their sales, before actually collecting the money from customers.

You would expect that if a company's sales were growing, then the account receivables would also grow. In order to tell whether accounts receivable growth is getting out of hand, you should compare it with the growth in sales (which we will talk about in the next chapter). Ideally, the growth of accounts receivable should be less than or equal to the growth in sales.

Inventory

Inventory is the raw materials or the finished goods the company needs to produce whatever it sells. In the SportsTee example, the inventory is basically the raw T-shirts. Increasing inventory is good only if the company expects to make and sell more items in the near future. For the most part, however, increasing inventory levels sometimes signal that the company is not selling enough of the products it makes. An increase in inventory is usually a bad sign.

Accounts Payable

In general, an increasing accounts payable balance can be a good thing because this means that the company is delaying making payments to those it owes money. By delaying payments, it is more or less getting a loan at a low rate for a short period of time.

Think of your parents' credit card payments. When your parents use their charge cards to make a $100 purchase, they effectively create an accounts payable of $100 on their personal balance sheet. They will have to pay the credit card company $100 when the bill is due. If they choose to, they can send a $100 check to the credit card company the next day after making the purchase in order to pay for the purchase before the bill arrives at your house. But why should they pay the bill so quickly when the credit card company will probably not bill them for the charge until the end of the month? They can probably use that $100 for their immediate needs and wait for the bill to come. In this way, they are effectively getting an interest-free loan from the credit card company for the number of days it will take for the bill to reach your house.

An increasing accounts payable due to the fact that the company can't pay its bills could mean trouble. But this trouble may show up in your current ratio calculation anyway. For a relatively stable company, rising accounts payable is a good thing.

HAS THE COMPANY BORROWED TOO MUCH?

The next important question that the balance sheet can answer is whether the company has borrowed too much money. On a personal level, you probably know that it is not a good thing to owe lots of money. For one thing, the bigger your debt, the more of your allowance or salary you would have to use to pay people back. Of course this means you would have less money to spend on the things that are really important to you.

Many investors also look at the amount of debt owed by companies to determine whether these companies are good long-term investments. Typically, investors consider the *debt-equity ratio*, which is simply long-term debt divided by equity (including preferred stock, common stock and retained earnings). SportsTee's debt-equity ratio is .16 ($400/$2,500). Hewlett-Packard Company and General Motors Corporation had debt-equity ratios of .05 and 4.91, respectively, at the time of this writing. As you can see from these numbers, different industries have different standards of how much debt is normal. The computer and electronics business typically has much smaller debt-equity ratios than the automobile business. Therefore, it is important to compare the debt levels in companies in the same industries. In general, however, all things being equal, less debt is better than more debt.

We recommend that beginning investors invest in companies that have a debt-equity ratio of less than or equal to .50. If a Teenvestor is interested in an industry that has traditionally high debt-equity ratios, she should choose companies with the lowest debt-equity ratios in that industry. In addition, it is best to calculate a debt-equity ratio over several years to see whether it is increasing or decreasing. It is usually a good thing when debt-equity ratios are going down over time. You will find more information about debt-equity ratios in Chapter 13.

WHAT IS THE COMPANY WORTH IF IT GOES BANKRUPT?

The balance sheet can also tell you the value of the company if it were to go bankrupt. This "value" is called *book value* and it can be illustrated with SportsTee. Book value represents the difference of the assets and liabilities on the balance sheet:

Book Value = Assets − Liabilities

It represents what the company is worth when it sells all its assets and pays off all its liabilities. (Note that this is also equal to Equity). Using the balance sheet on Table 3, Book Value = $3,500 - $1,000 = $2,500. The *book value per share* is the book value divided by the number of shares outstanding. SportsTee's book value per share is $500 ($2,500 book value/5 shares). Book value per share differs from *market value per share* in one very important respect: market value per share is the price you will find in the newspapers or on financial websites for a particular stock. Book value simply looks at the value of the company here and now if the company closed down for business.

The way investors typically use book value is to compare it with market value. They reason that if a company has a book value that is more than its market value, then chances are that the stock is under priced and its market value will probably go up.

In general, book value gives some indication of the financial health of manufacturing companies with significant fixed assets. All things being equal, when comparing two companies with significant *tangible assets* (assets you can touch and feel) in the same type of business, the company whose book value is above its market value would probably make a better investment. The problems with book values and balance sheets in general are explored in the next section.

WHAT THE BALANCE SHEET CANNOT REVEAL

The balance sheet is only one of the items investors look at when it comes time to evaluate a company to see whether buying its stock will make a good investment. It is probably not the most important tool for looking at all companies. It is fine for looking at some companies that manufacture things, but not necessarily good for looking at companies that provide information because these companies' assets are primarily the "brain power" or the know-how they offer their customers. For example, the main assets of any newspapers and magazines are its writers who use their intellectual skills to craft good articles. In addition, some Internet companies, which offer their technological know-how can't be evaluated simply by looking at their balance sheets. We will discuss how to evaluate such technology companies in a later chapter.

Even for manufacturing companies, one good example of how balance sheet analysis can break down is with book value. In our opinion, investors put too much faith in the practice of using book value as an indicator of a bargain. One shortcoming of book value is that assets on the balance sheet do not include intangible assets—assets such as intellectual capacity (the brain) and brand name that one can't really put a value on. For example, the most important asset possessed by a company that writes and produces software is its people—those who use the various computer languages to come up with innovative computer packages such as Microsoft Excel or Word. There is no way to properly value people when they produce items like software. Another example where the tangible assets of the company may not necessarily reflect the true value of its assets is the McDonald's Corporation. Any company can sell hamburgers but if a company can get golden arches and a McDonald's sign in front of its store (with permission from McDonald's, of course), it will immediately command a certain amount of respect from people walking by its store. The value of the McDonald's name is not reflected in the tally of its assets when its book value is calculated.

Even for companies whose assets are primarily tangible assets, there is one major shortcoming: book value can be misleading because the value of an asset you see on many balance sheets is not really the true value you would get for those assets if you wanted to sell them today. The value of the assets on a balance sheet is called *historical value* while the true value of an asset is called *market value*. Suppose, for example, that the value under Property, Plant, and Equipment on the SportsTee balance sheet on Table 5.1 was really worth $280, the current value, instead of $680, the historical value shown on the balance sheet. This would have made the total asset balance of $3,100 as opposed to an asset balance of $3,500. The total book value would have been $2,100 ($3,100 in assets less $1,000 in liabilities) therefore the book value per share would have been $420 per share versus $500 per share as previously calculated. You can see that when the value of Property, Plant, and Equipment is adjusted from $680 to $280, the book value per share goes down by $80 per share.

Note that depreciation plays a prominent role in the book value of a company. Since depreciation reduces the value of the fixed assets on the balance sheet, it tends to reduce book value. But what if a company applies less depreciation than it should on the fixed assets? For example, SportsTee could theoretically show the bucket with its original value of $120 on the balance sheet after one year even though, as we saw in the previous section, the depreciation of the bucket reduces its value to $90 in that time frame. By proper depreciation not being applied, the book value of SportsTee would be calculated as $30 higher than it should be.

All this is to say that book value can vary depending on how the assets on the balance sheet are valued. Therefore, it is not always a reliable measure of the value of the company if it breaks up.

ASSIGNMENT 5.1 TO 5.3

Assignment 5.1:Calculate the current ratio for the following balance sheets for two companies—Company X and Company Y. If the companies were exactly alike (in that they earn the same amount of money) except for their balance sheets, which one would you rather lend money today?

	Company X	Company Y
Current Assets	$1,000	$1,000
Fixed Assets	$300	$900
Total Assets	**$1,300**	**$1,900**
Current Liabilities	$500	$1,100
Long-Term Liab.	$200	$100
Equity	$600	$700
Total Liab. + Equity	**$1,300**	**$1,900**

Assignment 5.2: On our website, www.teenvestor.com, in the section for this chapter, you will see two balance sheets for the Ford Motor Company and The Microsoft Corporation. What are the differences in the two balance sheets? Compare the fixed assets and depreciation of the two companies. Which is bigger?

ASSIGNMENT 5.1 TO 5.3 CONT'D

Assignment 5.3: Tell us which of the following things is generally a good or bad thing for a company.

1. Cash goes up.
2. Retained Earnings goes up.
3. Accounts Receivable goes up.
4. Accounts Payable goes up.
5. Current Ratio goes down.
6. Inventory keeps growing.

Our website, www.teenvestor.com, will give you more information about balance

sheet numbers and how they can be used to gauge how well a company is do-

6

INCOME STATEMENT BASICS

An *income statement* shows the amount of money a company takes in, the expenses of the company, and the *net earnings* (also know as *net profit*, *net income*, or just plain *earnings*) of the company over a specific period of time. The net income or net earnings is the amount of money the company has left after paying its expenses and its taxes. Table 6.1, on the next page, shows SportsTee's income statement for a one-year period. The company's net earnings for a one-year period, as shown in Table 6.1, were based on the number and sales price of shirts sold during the year, the cost of the shirts, the other expenses associated with the business, and the taxes paid by the company. We will describe each of these components in detail. Follow the numbers on the side of the income statement.

TABLE 6.1
SportsTee's Income Statement
(At The End Of The First Year Of Operation)

1.	Number of Shirts Sold	1,200
2.	Sales Price Of Each Shirt	$15
3.	Total Revenue (#1 Times #2)	$18,000
4.	Total Cost of Raw (Unpainted) Shirts	($3,600)
5.	Cost Of Paint & Brushes & Overalls	($2,650)
6.	Depreciation Of Bucket	($30)
7.	Rental Of Space Per Year	($1,200)
8.	Advertising	($600)
9.	Total Labor By All 5 Owners	($7,200)
10.	Interest On Loan (10% On loan)	($100)
11.	Total Expenses (Sum Of #4 To #10)	($15,380)
12.	Earnings Before Taxes (#3 Less #11)	$2,620
13.	Tax (#12 Times 40%)	$1,048
14.	**Net Earnings (#12 Less #13)**	**$1,572**

The line numbers below describe some components of Table 6.1:

#1 Shirts Sold—the amount of shirts sold by Susan and her four partners during the year. Here, Susan and her friends sold 1,200 shirts.

#2 Sales Price—the sales price for each of the shirts. Here, the shirt is sold for $15 each.

#3 *Revenue* (also known as Sales) is the amount of money taken in by a company when it sells its goods. In this case, Total Revenue is the product of the total number of shirts sold and the sales price for each shirt: (1,200 shirts) x ($15 per shirt) = $18,000.

#11 These are the sum of the expense items for SportsTee (items #4 to #10). Pay particular attention to the depreciation and the interest rate figures (# 6 and #10). Because we assume the bucket will wear out in four years, we have to recognize as an expense, the portion of the bucket that is used up each year—in other words, $1/4^{th}$ of the bucket, or $30. The interest is the amount of interest that has to be paid on the money borrowed to start the business.

#12 to #14 *Earnings Before Taxes* (#12) is the amount of money the company takes in less the expenses of the company. #13 is the amount of taxes the company pays on the Earnings Before Taxes. #14 is the *Net Earnings* (or *Net Income* or *Net Profit*)—what is left after paying everything you owe, including taxes.

There are really three main components of the income statement: Total Revenue (line #3), Total Expenses (line #11), Net Earnings (line #14). In general, investors look at the growth of Net Earnings as it relates to the amount of shares in the company.

Corporations usually release their earnings for each three-month interval during its *fiscal year*. These are called *quarterly earnings*. A fiscal year is the one-year period in which the company measures its performance. This period can be from January 1 to December 31 or any other one-year period such as from February 1 to January 31. In fact a company can define its fiscal year as beginning in any month and ending twelve months later. A company that has its fiscal year beginning on January 1 will release quarterly earnings for the following periods: January 1 to March 31, April 1 to June 30, July 1 to September 30, and October 1 to December 31. On the other hand, a company with a fiscal year that begins on February 1 will release quarterly earnings for the following periods: February 1 to April 30, May 1 to July 31, August 1 to October 30, and November 1 to January 31.

Stock analysts compare earnings from one quarter to the corresponding previous year's quarter. This type of comparison is reasonable because some businesses are seasonal. That is, sales in some quarters are bigger than in others. In the case of SportsTee, Susan and her friends may find that their T-shirts are more popular in May, when it starts to warm up in the Northeast, than in January, when it is cold. It makes sense for SportsTee to compare sales in the current period with the same period in a previous year. This practice is even more justified with retail stores because many of them make 30% to 40% of their year's sales during the Christmas holiday season. It makes perfect sense for these stores to compare sales of one Christmas season with the previous Christmas season.

Our website, www.teenvestor.com, will give you more information about income statements.

7

WHAT THE INCOME STATEMENT REVEALS

The income statement can reveal a lot of information that investors can use to make decisions on what stocks to buy. In this chapter, we will show you how to use some of this information to understand a company's profitability.

EARNING PER SHARE

One very important figure most investors look at is how much profit each shareholder makes for each dollar he or she invests. This is usually called *earnings per share* and it is calculated by dividing after-tax earnings by the number of shares issued by the company. For the SportsTee example, this can be calculated by dividing its net earnings, $1,572 (as calculated in the previous chapter) by the 5 shares held by Susan and her partners. This calculation, $1,572/5, is equal to $314.40 earned per share. The latest available full-year earnings per share for International Business Machines Corporation

(IBM) and the McDonald's Corporation at the time of this writing were $4.12 and $1.40, respectively. These companies have smaller earnings-per-share figures than SportsTee because such giant corporations have a lot of shares outstanding. As we mentioned in a previous chapter, Ford Motor Company's most recent year-end common shares in the hands of investors stands at about 1,910,000,000 shares.

An earnings per share, or EPS as it's commonly called, is more meaningful when you look at EPS growth from period to period and when you compare it with the EPS of other companies in the same line of business. We will discuss EPS in full in Chapter 13.

NET PROFIT MARGIN

In addition to EPS, another way to measure how profitable a company was in any given year is through its *net profit margin* (also known as profit margin). Net profit margin is a company's net earnings divided by its total revenue. For SportsTee, the revenue was $18,000 and the net earnings were $1,572, so the calculation of net profit margin (in percentage terms) is as follows:

$$\text{Net Profit Margin} = \$1{,}572 \times 100 / 18{,}000 = 8.7\%$$

What this means is that SportsTee kept only 8.7% of the revenue it took in during the year. This number is useful only when you compare it to the net profit margin of the same company in prior years or you compare it to the net profit margin of other companies in the same business as SportsTee.

Big corporations also have tiny net profit margins. This is always a big surprise to Teenvestors who, like most people, think that companies keep a lot more money than they do. Ford Motor Company, for example, had a year-end net profit margin of about 2% (due to some unusual expenses) at the time of this writing. This meant that out of a revenue figure of $170 billion, it kept about $3.5 billion—a big sum of money, but not so big when you compare it to the company's revenue.

DIVIDENDS AND RETAINED EARNINGS

After a company determines how much money it has made during the year, it has to decide what to do with that money. It can do basically two things with the money: pay it all to its shareholders or plow it back into the company to buy equipment or expand the business. The biggest companies in America such as IBM and McDonald's often pay some of the profits to shareholders as *dividends* and also to keep some of the money in the company. The money kept in the company is called *retained earnings* and you will find it under the equity section of the balance sheet. You can think of retained earnings as additional equity that the owners of the company have contributed to the business.

Table 7.1, on the next page, shows that even though SportsTee made $1,572 after taxes during the year, it distributed only $1,000 to the 5 Teenvestors that own the business. Therefore, each partner actually received $200 ($200 = $1,000 / 5). The remaining $572 was put back into the company and it can be viewed as the additional money the 5 investors put into the company above and beyond their original investment of $500 each.

TABLE 7.1
Effect Of Paying Dividends
(Retained Earnings)

Earnings Before Taxes	=	$2,620
Net Earnings (After Paying 40% Tax On Earnings)	=	$1,572
Net Earnings Paid As Dividends	=	($1,000)
Net Earnings Retained In Company	=	**$572**

The $572, which represents retained earnings, is added to the original equity investment of $2,500 ($500 per partner x 5 = $2,500) for a total equity balance of $3,072. The lesson here is that profits not distributed as dividends represent additional investments by the shareholders.

THE DIVIDEND YIELD

The *dividend yield*, the ratio of the dividend per share to the price of each share, is another frequently watched figure in the stock-picking game. The dividend per share for each SportsTee stockholder is $200 ($200 = $1,000 / 5 shareholders). Therefore, the dividend yield is 40% ($200/$500), since the dividend per share is $200 and the price of each share owned by the SportsTee partners is $500.

Most companies pay out a fixed dollar amount of dividends per share from year to year, with occasional adjustments. For many investors, dividend yield is important because it provides them with a steady source of income above the possible appreciated value of the stock. But when you think about it, a high dividend yield could mean that the share price has gone down which could mean a loss to you when it is time to sell. For example, buying stock based on dividend yield can also be faulty because companies that are not doing well can easily cut or eliminate their dividends. The lesson here is that dividend yields can vary greatly because they depend on share prices and the economic conditions that companies are facing.

The stocks of stable, well-established companies that have paid dividends to investors over a long period of time and that are no longer growing at a fast pace are known *as blue-chip stocks*. When Teenvestors begin investing, they should start with shares in these types of companies. However, as they gain more experience as investors, we also recommend that they gradually buy shares in faster growing companies that pay no dividends but instead, plow all their profits back into the company to help the company thrive. The stocks of these types of companies are known as *growth stocks*. To illustrate why growth stocks can be desirable, take another look at SportsTee. Recall that the company paid out $1,000 in dividends to the 5 shareholders. If you were looking at investing in SportsTee wouldn't you prefer to see that the company is plowing back all its earnings into the company in order to buy new equipment, do more advertising, and spend money trying to nurture the company? We would because we know that the company is laying the groundwork to really do well in the future. This is how Teenvestors should be thinking. They should seek to hold in their *portfolios* (their bags of investments) some shares of these types of growth-oriented stocks. But a majority of their shares should remain blue-chip stocks until they become super-advance investors.

Our website, www.teenvestor.com, will give you more information about how to get good information from income statements.

8

UNDERSTANDING THE MARKET

The Market. You hear the term being used on the evening financial news. It is mentioned in the daily newspapers. Your parents may even talk about it. But do you know what it really means?

Without getting into a precise definition, the phrase "the market" usually refers to the stock market. When people ask about the condition of the market, they are asking whether prices of stocks are generally increasing or decreasing.

Knowing that the market exists is one thing, but knowing how to measure the health of the market is another thing. In the U.S. economy, experts have come up with ways to measure the market. In this chapter, we will discuss the marketplace where stocks are bought and sold, and the various measures that are used by investors to tell how well the market is doing.

WHERE STOCK IS BOUGHT AND SOLD

Stocks are bought and sold through *exchanges*—institutions such as the New York Stock Exchange (NYSE), the American Stock Exchange (AMEX), and the National Association of Securities Dealers Automated Quotation System (NASDAQ) through which stockbrokers trade (in other words, buy and sell) stock. Each of these exchanges has its own rules and regulations that govern which companies can be listed on the exchange.

Launched in 1817, the New York Stock Exchange lists some of the biggest companies in the country. The American Stock Exchange, which was launched in 1842, is commonly viewed as the younger sibling of the New York Stock Exchange. NASDAQ was started in 1971 as the exchange for smaller companies, but it has grown to include such big companies as Microsoft, Intel, and MCI.

You don't have to know whether a stock is traded on the NYSE, AMEX, or NASDAQ when you buy or sell stock. Your stockbroker or your online broker will simply buy the shares for you—they are the ones who have to know where to go to acquire the shares.

At the end of each day, these exchanges record what is known as *closing prices* for each stock. Closing prices are generally the last price during the day at which the stock was bought or sold. The closing prices in these exchanges are what are often used to tell if the stock market is doing well or not.

STOCK MARKET INDICATORS YOU SHOULD KNOW

An indicator is a number that gives you an idea of the qualities that you are trying to measure. For example, let's say that you want an easy way to gauge how the temperature in your town changes from day to day without having to measure the temperature yourself. One way to do this is to find out the temperature in, say, 10 locations around the boundary of your county and divide by ten. This average would probably be a good approximation of the temperature in your town. Obviously, to get a more precise number, you would have to measure the temperature in a lot more than 10 locations in your county. The average temperature of these ten spots is now your indicator or *index* for your town's temperature. You can call it anything you want: The Teenvestor Temperature Index, The TTI, or whatever you like. If this index is calculated and published every day by some organization, you can get an approximation on how the temperature in your town changes by looking at the changes in the index alone.

The following are the three important stock market indicators or indexes most stock experts use to tell how stocks are doing: The Dow Jones Industrial Average (The Dow or The DJIA), The Standard & Poor's 500 (The S&P 500), and the NASDAQ Composite Index (The NASDAQ Composite).

The Dow Jones Industrial Average

The most prominent stock market indicator in the United States is The Dow. Charles Henry Dow first published the Dow on May 26, 1896. At that time, it included the sum of the prices of just 12 so-called "smoke stack" companies, such as coal and gas companies. Today, The Dow is made up of 30 stocks of some of the biggest companies in America. Table 8.1, on page 107, lists the companies that are included in The Dow. The stocks for The Dow are pulled primarily from the New York Stock Exchange. Of the original 12 stocks included in The Dow, General Electric is the only company still on the list.

The index is calculated by summing up the "adjusted prices" of the stocks of the companies listed on the table. The adjusted prices are the stock price for each company, adjusted for things such as *stock splits* (further explained in our website). You won't be able to calculate The Dow on your own by averaging all the closing prices of the 30 stocks that make up The Dow, without knowing how to adjust the price of each stock. But Teenvestors shouldn't really care about how The Dow is calculated. All that should matter to them is whether the index goes up or down, and by how much.

When you hear on the evening news or read in your local newspaper that The Dow went up 20 points, you can think of it as meaning that the average of the stock prices in The Dow went up by $20. Sometimes the change in The Dow is given in percentage terms such as "The Dow was up 15% yesterday." As long as you know in what terms the change is expressed—whether in points or in percentage—you can gauge the seriousness of the change in The Dow.

Many investors focus on the day-to-day changes in The Dow. As a Teenvestor, you shouldn't be concerned with daily changes because you are a long-term investor. You are in stocks for the long haul—four, five, seven years and beyond. As long as you've done your research on a company, and feel good about its long-term prospects, declines or increases in The Dow should not get you overly excited.

TABLE 8.1
The 30 Companies In The Dow Jones Industrial Average

Alcoa Inc.
American Express Co.
AT&T Corp.
Boeing Co.
Caterpillar Inc.
Citigroup Inc.
Coca-Cola Co.
DuPont (E.I.) de Nemours & Co.
Eastman Kodak
Exxon Mobil Corp.
General Electric Co.
General Motors
Hewlett-Packard Co.
Home Depot Inc.
Honeywell International Inc.
Intel Corp.
International Business Machines Corp. (IBM)
International Paper Co.
J.P. Morgan Chase & Co.
Johnson & Johnson
McDonald's Corp.
Merck & Co. Inc.
Microsoft Corp.
Minnesota Mining & Mfg. Co. (3M)
Philip Morris Cos.
Procter & Gamble Co.
SBC Communications Inc.
United Technologies Corp.
Wal-Mart Stores Inc.
Walt Disney Co.

The Dow has been criticized because it measures how big companies are doing and because it does not include some of the types of businesses that now play a role in the economic life of the country. For example, an Internet company like America Online (AOL) is currently not on The Dow. What this means is that The Dow does not look much like the portfolio of stocks held by many small investors—especially those investors who like high technology growth stocks.

To partially respond to this criticism, four companies were removed from The Dow—Chevron Corp., Goodyear Tire & Rubber, Sears Roebuck & Co., and Union Carbide Corp.,—and replaced by Microsoft Corp., Intel Corp., Home Depot, and SBC Communications in 1999. This was the most sweeping change in The Dow in a long time. The Dow remains the oldest and most quoted index of the American stock market.

Table 8.2 on the next page shows the year-end levels of The Dow (and other stock market indicators) from 1989 to 2000. At the time of this writing, the highest level ever reached by The Dow is 11,908.50.

ASSIGNMENT 8.1 TO 8.2

Assignment 8.1: On our site, www.teenvestor.com, you will find a link to the site that will give you the value of The Dow for any dates you want. Find the value for The Dow on the last trading day of the following years: 1917, 1927, 1937, 1947, 1957, 1967, 1977, 1987, and 1997.

Assignment 8.2: Calculate the value of The Dow for the latest trading day. Our site, www.teenvestor.com, will show you how to calculate it for any trading day.

TABLE 8.2
The Level Of The Dow, The S&P 500, And The NASDAQ*
(Figures Are For The Last Trading Day Of Each Year)

	The Dow	S&P 500	NASDAQ
2000	10,786.85	1,320.28	2,470.52
1999	11,497.12	1,469.25	4,069.30
1998	9,181.43	1,229.23	2,192.69
1997	7,908.43	970.43	1,570.35
1996	6,448.27	740.74	1,291.03
1995	5,117.12	615.93	1,052.13
1994	3,834.44	459.27	751.96
1993	3,754.09	466.45	776.80
1992	3,301.11	435.71	676.95
1991	3,168.83	417.09	586.34
1990	2,633.66	330.22	373.84
1989	2,753.20	353.40	454.82

*Updates At www.teenvestor.com as Data Becomes Available

The S&P 500

Another gauge investors use to tell how the market is doing is the Standard & Poor's 500. As the name suggests, there are 500 stocks in this index. The stocks in this index are too numerous to list here but it includes many of the stocks found in The Dow, and many more stocks—at least 470 more stocks. The stocks in the S&P 500 Index are traded on the NYSE, the AMEX and the NASDAQ exchanges. Since the S&P 500 has more stocks in it and covers many more types of businesses than The Dow, it is considered a better measure of how the stock market is doing.

Like The Dow, the change in the S&P 500 is at times given in terms of points (dollar amounts) and at times in terms of percentage.

Table 8.2 shows the year-end levels of The S&P 500 (and other stock market indicators) from 1989 to 2000. At the time of this writing, the highest level ever reached by the S&P 500 is 1,553.11.

The NASDAQ Composite

The NASDAQ Composite Index (The NASDAQ) is made up of the thousands of stocks traded on the NASDAQ exchange.

Recall that in an earlier section we told you that the NASDAQ Exchange is generally where the stocks of smaller, lesser-known companies are traded. For this reason, the NASDAQ Composite Index is used to tell how smaller companies are doing. Of late, The NASDAQ has been doing well because of small high-technology companies that have had huge run-ups in stock prices.

Like The Dow, the change in the NASDAQ Composite Index is given in terms of points (dollar amounts) and in terms of percentage.

Table 8.2 shows the year-end levels of the NASDAQ Composite Index (and other stock market indicators) from 1989 to 2000. At the time of this writing, the highest level ever reached by the NASDAQ Composite Index is 5,048.62.

How The Dow, The S&P 500, And The NASDAQ Composite Are Related

As you can imagine, there is a relationship between The Dow, The S&P 500, and the NASDAQ Composite since they are all supposed to give an indication of what is happening in the stock market. In general, when one moves up, the others move up as well. The point increase or percentage increase may be different, however, because of the types of stocks included in the various indexes. Because The Dow includes the stocks of the biggest companies in the country, it tends not to move up or down as much as The S&P 500 and the NASDAQ Composite. Just think of The Dow as a big ship that is hard to slow down or speed up.

Even though, in general, the three indexes move up and down together, there are times when the NASDAQ Composite is out of step with The Dow and The S&P 500. This happened quite frequently in 1999 and 2000. The reason was that technology stocks were primarily what determined the NASDAQ Composite. These stocks were red hot at that time, regardless of what was happening to the rest of the stocks in the stock market.

Other Indices

There are many more indexes that investors use in determining how the stock market is doing. Some investors may put their money in specific types of businesses such as Internet-related, Oil/Gasoline-related, or Transportation-related businesses, so they need indexes that tell them how those businesses are doing in general. Such indexes *do* exist. We won't go through all of them here but when you become a more advanced Teenvestor, you can look them all up if you need them. For now, the three major indexes—The Dow, The S&P 500, and the NASDAQ Composite—are all you need to know.

> Our website, www.teenvestor.com, will give you more information about major United States indexes as well as indexes of other countries.

9

GOVERNMENT INFORMATION AND ACTIONS THAT AFFECT THE MARKET

The government publishes lots of information to tell the public how the economy is doing. Some investors use this information as a basis for deciding whether to keep their money in the stock market or move it to other investments they consider safer or more profitable. This chapter discusses how financial information and actions by the U.S. Government affect the behavior of investors.

GOVERNMENT INFORMATION

Information about how fast prices are going up, the amount of products American industries make and sell, and how many people have jobs, are some of the most important things that affect the stock market. In this section, we will show you how these factors make stock prices go up and down.

Inflation And The Consumer Price Index (CPI)

In general, *inflation* is the extent to which your money today will buy less in the future. You have probably come face-to-face with inflation at some point in your life. For example, you may have noticed that the price of a movie ticket has gone up, or that the cost of your favorite food items has increased. There are many reasons why prices go up:

1. Inflation can be caused because more people want a particular product. For example, on Valentine's Day, roses are more expensive because husbands and boyfriends want to buy them for their loved ones.

2. Inflation can be caused by companies raising prices in response to the increase in the amount of money it takes to make the products they are selling to the public. For example, car prices went up slightly when automobile companies were required by law to include air bags in cars.

3. Inflation can be caused by planned shortages. For example, if the companies that produce the oil used to make gasoline decide to cut back on the amount of oil they ship to customers (as they did in the early 1970s and 1980s, way before you were born), this could increase the price of oil.

4. Inflation can be caused by fear of shortages. For example, during a war, certain items such as oil may go up in price because people are scared their supplies will be cut off.

The *Consumer Price Index* or CPI is one measure of inflation used by the government. The U.S. Labor Department produces the monthly CPI, which measures the increase in the price of a given "basket" of goods and services purchased by typical consumers. It covers a large number of items, including food, housing, apparel, transportation, medical care, and entertainment.

A very simplified example of how the CPI calculation works is that prices are added together for the typical items people buy and this sum is compared to the same "basket" of goods a year later. For example, a basket of goods could include things like milk, gas, meat, rent, clothes, and other things essential for everyday life. Adding up the prices of these items one year and adding up the prices a year later can tell you whether prices are moving up or down. The percentage increase in price for these goods will be the inflation number. Of course, prices can also go down, too, in which case you've got *deflation*.

Inflation is given in percentage terms. At the time of this writing, the inflation rate reflected in the CPI, was about 3.4%. You can interpret this number to mean that, in general, basic items cost 3.4% more today than a year ago. The highest inflation rate based on the CPI was 18% in 1918 and the lowest was negative 10.5% in 1921.

To understand how inflation affects the stock market, you first have to understand what determines stock prices of the companies traded on the various exchanges we discussed earlier. The stock price of a company depends on how much that company is expected to make in the future. To make it perfectly clear, net earnings (also known as net income and net profit) drive a company's stock price. In other words, the more you expect a company to earn in the future, the higher the value of the company's stock.

If inflation is high, a company's earnings in the future are worth less and less. That's because what the company earns in the future can't buy the same things it can buy today. If a company's future earnings are worth less in the future, then its stock price will go down. Therefore, in general, the higher the inflation, the worse things are for the stock market. The relationship between stock prices and inflation is further explained in Chapter 10.

To show you a real example of how inflation rate (as reflected in the consumer price index) affects the stock market, here is an excerpt from the April 17, 2000 edition of *The Wall Street Journal*:

> Stocks plunged, with the major indexes enduring their biggest point drops ever and among their steepest percentage losses in a decade. Friday's *consumer-price* report indicated that inflation was resurfacing. The Nasdaq Composite Index dropped 355.49 points, or 9.7%, to 3,321.29. The Dow Jones industrials sank 617.78 points to 10,305.77.

This passage above was referring to one of the biggest-ever point drops in the market—for both The Dow and the NASDAQ—that occurred on Friday, April 14, 2000. This drop was caused primarily by a consumer price index report, which showed that inflation jumped by .7%

Inflation also affects the *interest rate* on borrowing money. (Interest rates are the fees you pay for borrowing money). The higher the inflation rate, the higher the interest rate you will pay in order to borrow money. This is because lenders want to make up for the fact that the higher inflation will make the interest paid them by borrowers worth less and less. So, to make up for these losses, they have to increase the amount of interest they are paid.

Gross Domestic Product

Gross Domestic Product (GDP) is the dollar value of what the national economy produced during a certain period. You can think of it as the report card for the United States. The GDP includes the following items:

1. How much you, your family, and other citizens spend on items such as food, clothing, services, and other items.

2. The money businesses spend to buy equipment for their factories, the money families spend to buy homes, and the change in certain items on the balance sheet of companies.

3. The money spent by the government for defense, roads, schools, and other items.

4. The amount of goods and services the United States sells to other countries.

Of all the items listed above, the biggest contributor to the GDP is item 1—how much you, your family, and other citizens spend on items such as food, clothing, services, and other items.

You will rarely see the actual dollar amount of GDP printed anywhere. What you are likely to see is the percentage GDP growth. The growth figure is watched very carefully to check the health of the economy. In the past, the typical GDP growth rate has been between 2.5% and 3.0%.

A fast-growing GDP can lead to inflation because this probably means that too many consumers are buying goods and services. (When you have more people with more money trying to buy goods and services, prices tend to go up). When the GDP does not grow but instead declines, this is known as a *recession*. The way the government tries to cure too much inflation or a recession is to change an interest rate called the *discount rate* in order to affect how much money people borrow and spend. This process is described later in this chapter.

The Employment Report

There are a certain number of people in the United States who have jobs (or *the employed*, as they are known) at any particular point in time. There are also a certain number of people who are actively seeking jobs (or *the unemployed*, as they are known). These numbers change from time to time, but in May 2001, the number of employed people stood at about 135,103,000 while the unemployed numbered 6,169,000. The Employment Report, published monthly by the U.S. Department of Labor, provides the employment and unemployment numbers. Together, the number of people employed and the number of people unemployed make up the *labor force* or *workforce*. The labor force number was 141,272,000 in May 2001. The *unemployment rate* is the percentage of the workforce that is out of work. In 2000, the unemployment rate hit a landmark low of 4.1%—the lowest rate since 1970. The May 2001 unemployment rate was 4.4% (6,169,000 / 141,272,000). The highest unemployment rate at the time of this writing was 10.8% in 1982. The lowest unemployment rate was 2.5% in 1953.

People who are not employed and are not seeking employment are not counted as part of the workforce. Usually, rising employment and declining unemployment are signs of an improving economy.

Most beginning Teenvestors think that a low unemployment rate is good for the stock market. In their minds, it is wonderful when everyone has a job. They are shocked to discover that when an Employment Report shows that the unemployment rate is lower than expected, the stock market actually goes down under normal circumstances. In other words, The Dow, The S&P 500, and the NASDAQ Composite Index generally go down in value. Likewise, when the Employment Report comes out which shows that the unemployment rate is higher than expected, the stock market generally improves.

The explanation for the stock market's reaction to the Employment Report is that when the unemployment rate is lower than expected, it means that more people are working. If more people are working, it also means that more people are going to be spending money, and contributing to the GDP. As is sometimes the case, when more people are spending money, the stock market is scared of that dreaded "I" word—inflation. Inflation fears usually causes the stock market to go down.

For young investors, this is a hard thing to accept because while they want the stock market to do well, they also don't want to rejoice when more people are out of work. The only way Teenvestors can feel better about this is to realize that high inflation can cause the quality of life for tens of millions of Americans to decrease in ways that are not always obvious. For example, an increase in mortgage rates (the interest rates that people pay on money they have borrowed to buy their houses) which is caused by inflation could cost home owners a few hundred dollars more a month, could discourage people from buying homes in the first place, or could disqualify people who want to borrow money to buy a home. Skyrocketing heating oil prices could mean that some people may not be able to afford oil to keep warm in their homes during winter.

THE GOVERNMENT ACTIONS THAT AFFECTS
THE ECONOMY

If the GDP is growing too fast, it means primarily that consumers are spending a lot of money (because consumer spending makes up the majority of the GDP). As you have already learned, when a lot of people with a lot of money are trying to buy the same goods, this typically results in inflation. (Recall that we discussed how on Valentine's Day roses are more expensive because more people want roses on that day). Things, in general, become more expensive when too many consumers have money (either money from their jobs or money they have borrowed) to buy these items.

To stop consumers and others who contribute to the GDP from spending too much money too fast, the government (specifically, the Federal Reserve Bank) makes it harder for people to borrow money by increasing the *discount rate*. This increase, which is known as "the tightening of monetary policy," eventually makes it more expensive for consumers and others to borrow money from banks. With less money being borrowed, there is less spending. This eventually reduces consumer spending, reduces the possibility of inflation, and causes the GDP to go down.

If the GDP is not growing at all, it probably means that consumers are not spending much money. To encourage people to spend more money, the Federal Reserve Bank can decrease the discount rate, which eventually makes it easier for consumers to borrow money. This action is known as "loosening monetary policy."

You might be puzzled as to why the Federal Reserve Bank has to interfere in the economy in the first place. The first question you might be asking yourself is why the Federal Reserve will raise rates to stop inflation. The best way to think about the Federal Reserve's action is to think of the economy as a train that is to pick up passengers at various locations at specific times. A train that is going too fast can derail and crash. This is what happens when the economy is too hot because of high inflation. Much like the motorman of the train who taps on the brakes to slow the train down, the Federal Reserve raises the discount rate to discourage people from borrowing and spending too much so as to slow down the economy and stop it from derailing.

If the train is going really slow, it will not meet its schedule. Much like the motorman who tinkers with the train's engine to increase its speed, the Federal Reserve stimulates the economy by reducing the discount rate in order to encourage more people to borrow and spend more money.

The following passage from *The Wall Street Journal* (June 9, 2000) summarizes some of the concepts we have been teaching regarding the economy and the Federal Reserve Bank's action to slow it down:

> The Nasdaq Composite Index gained 19% last week following a report that unemployment was rising and that businesses were eliminating jobs. That was bad news for job seekers, but it stirred hopes that the economy is slowing. If it starts seeing results from its yearlong campaign to cool the economy, the Fed might finally stop raising rates. Rising rates have been the main brake on the stock and bond markets.... While a slowing economy would help stocks, economic strength could send stocks down.

The excerpt below from *The New York Times* (June 27, 2001) gives a real-life example of how far the Federal Reserve Bank will go to jump-start a sluggish economy.

The Federal Reserve cut its benchmark interest rate by a quarter of a percentage point today and signaled that its campaign to revive the flagging economy may be entering its final stages. The rate cut was the sixth by the central bank since it became clear at the beginning of the year that the economy was slowing precipitously.... The move reduced the federal funds target rate on overnight loans among banks -- the Fed's primary tool for influencing the economy -- to 3.75 percent from 4 percent. The rate was last that low more than seven years ago.

The Federal Reserve's actions to keep the economy on an even keel make sense if you pause and give it some real thought. The only problem is that it is very difficult to know how fast or how long to apply the brakes on the economy or how much stimulation is needed to get the economy moving again.

HOW EXPECTATIONS DRIVE THE MARKET

The economy affects the stock market in many ways and the government produces lots of weekly, monthly and quarterly economic data to track and study it.

As we have just discussed, among the most important indicators are: inflation (the increase and decrease of prices), the gross domestic product or GDP (the sum of what goods and services are produced in the country), the unemployment rate (the number of people who can't find jobs), and the discount rate (the rate set by the government which eventually affects the interest rates your parents pay for borrowing money). These economic indicators are all related in one way or another. The stock market continuously adjusts itself by reassessing the value of stocks based on any new financial information it gets. The stock market also adjusts based on the guesses of financial experts on what the government's economic data and the government's action will be in the future.

As an example of how these indicators affect the stock market, let's examine the effect of the unemployment rate on the stock market. If, for example, investors think the unemployment rate for the next month will be 5% and it eventually proves to be 4%, there is a pretty good chance that the S&P 500 will go down. As we discussed earlier, the reason the stock market might go down in this case is that a lower unemployment rate could trigger inflation because it means that more people will have money to buy more goods and services. However, if the unemployment rate comes in at 5% as expected, a stock market index like the S&P 500 will probably not change much.

Real-life evidence of how expectations affect the market can be found, once again, in our earlier example of how the CPI affected the stock market on April 14, 2000. On that day, The Dow, and the NASDAQ Composite, dropped sharply because the newly released CPI showed a .7% increase. The major problem was not that the CPI increased, but that people expected an increase of only .5%. Here is how the April 17, 2000 issue of *Investor's Business Daily*, a leading financial newspaper, reported the drop in the market:

> Investor's got a rude awakening Friday. The consumer price index jumped .7% in March, the biggest gain in almost a year, casting already-weak stocks into another freefall. The surge was worse than the .5% rise most analysts expected.

As you can see, investors were disappointed that inflation was climbing higher than was expected, so they pulled their money out of the stock market. Of course, this helped cause the market to tumble.

Our website, www.teenvestor.com, will tell you how to get CPI, inflation, GDP, employment, unemployment, and labor force information. You will also find economic data about your state.

10

BUSINESS AND FINANCIAL CONCEPTS YOU SHOULD KNOW

You will feel a sense of satisfaction when you can listen to financial news on CNN or on Bloomberg and actually understand what they are talking about. With the concepts we explain in this chapter, you will learn some of the most important ideas all investors should know. After reading this chapter those financial news reporters will have nothing on you. In fact, you will probably know more than they do because many reporters just read the news, without understanding it. You, on the other hand, will have the benefit of knowing how the news affects the market.

Subsequent chapters in this book refer to some of the ideas explored here. We suspect that you will have to come back to this chapter again and again because it covers some of the most important business and financial concepts you will ever encounter.

SUPPLY & DEMAND

The law of *supply and demand* is an important idea in the stock market and in the course of everyday life. The principle of supply and demand states that if too many people want something, the price of that thing (whatever that thing is) will go up. (We briefly discussed this concept in the previous chapter and referred to increasing prices as inflation). The word "supply" usually refers to the availability of the product in question. The word "demand" usually refers to the desire to have that product. If there is too much supply of a product, that product becomes so common that the maker can't really charge too much for it.

Think of a stone like a diamond, which is a very expensive precious stone. One of the reasons diamonds are expensive is because the amount available for sale around the world is tightly controlled by a handful of dealers who create an artificial shortage. Because so many people want diamonds (for their weddings and for other special occasions) and because the supply is kept low, the price of diamonds stays high from year to year.

The prices of stocks also change according to how much is available and how much people want them. If more people want to sell a particular stock than to buy them, the price of that stock will fall because the stock market is truly a market with sellers (or those who supply stocks) and buyers (or those who want or demand stock).

THE TWO WAYS STOCKS CAN MAKE MONEY

Investors put their money into stocks because they want their
make money. The two ways stocks make money are
eipt of dividends, and through *capital appreciation*.

Dividends

Just to refresh your memory, dividends are the portion of a company's earnings that is paid to the investor every three months. Companies happily pay dividends when they make money. However, when profits are down or if these companies start losing money, they can decide to stop paying dividends.

The date a company announces the amount of dividends it will pay to its stockholders is called the *declaration date*. But not everyone who owns the company's stock will get the dividends the next time they are paid. It depends on when the shares were purchased. If an investor buys the shares by a date called the *ex-dividend date*, she will receive the current declared dividends. If she buys them just after the ex-dividend date, for example, she will start receiving dividends in about three months—the next time dividends are declared. The dividend is sent to the investor on a date called the *payment date*.

You may find that publishers, whether they are print or Internet-based publishers, report the yearly dividend of companies instead of the amount that is paid every quarter. So, a quarterly dividend of $.50 is reported as a $2.00 dividend—four times the quarterly dividend.

Capital Appreciation

Besides dividends, the only other way to make money with stocks is through *capital appreciation* or *capital gains* as it is sometimes known. Capital appreciation is the increase of the price of a stock.

THE RELATIONSHIP BETWEEN STOCKS AND BONDS

Even though this book is primarily about investing in stocks, you should be aware of the relationship between stocks and bonds. Just to refresh your memory, a stock represents a piece of a company owned by an investor, and a bond represents a loan to a company or to a government agency for which the lender receives interest payments.

In general, a company's bond is safer than its stock. By "safer" we mean that you are less likely to lose your money with bonds than with stocks when looking at investing in one company. As we discussed earlier, a riskier investment will pay you more than a safer investment. This is why the interest rates on some bonds are usually low compared with the amount of money you can make when the value of stocks go up. Of course, there is no guarantee that the value of the stock will go up at all. But this is part of the risk you take when you invest.

Many investors own both stocks and bonds. Sometimes they will switch their money from stocks to bonds and other times they will switch money from bonds to stocks. Exactly when they make the switch partially depends on inflation. This is because the interest rates paid on bonds depend on inflation—the higher the inflation rate, the more interest borrowers will have to pay lenders in order to make up for the fact that the payments they are making to these lenders will be eaten up by inflation. Therefore, the higher the interest rates, the more attractive bonds are to most investors looking for a safer place to put their money. This movement of money from stocks to bonds is known as *flight to quality* because investors seek safer, higher quality investments for their money.

investors keep track of what is happening in the bond a watchful eye on the U.S. government bond called the

30-year Treasury Bond, also known as the *long bond*. The interest rate or *yield* (as it is called) of this bond is published every day in financial newspapers and websites. When the yield goes up, investors know that inflation may be on its way. At the time of this writing, the yield on the long bond was 6.21%.

THE MEANING OF A BOND RALLY
(For The Advanced Teenvestor)

When you hear that the "stock market rallied," it means that stock prices have moved up. This is a good thing for those people who own stocks since they can benefit from the capital appreciation of these stocks.

But it is a bit more difficult to interpret the rally of the bond market. If you recall, a bond is basically a loan that pays interest. Corporate bonds usually pay interest twice a year to lenders.

If you own a 5-year corporate bond that pays you based on a loan of $1,000 at 10% interest, this means that you will get a total of $100 each year for 5 years. At the end of the fifth year, you will also get your original $1,000 back. Supposing that yesterday you bought this 5-year corporate bond for $1,000 (at an interest rate of 10%) but your friend buys a similar bond the next day but he gets a rate of only 9% because interest rates went down due to action by the Federal Reserve Bank between yesterday and today. Your bond is worth more because you are getting an interest rate of 10%, which is higher than the current rate of 9% any other bondholder will get if she purchased the same type of bond today.

The basic concept here is that once you own a bond that has a set interest rate, your bond looks better and better (i.e. it is worth more and more if you want to sell it) if interest rates go down. (Remember that your interest rate is already fixed so it won't go down as long as you own it). As rates goes down, your bond rallies or is worth more and more. To make a long story short, lower interest rates make bonds you own worth more. In other words, bonds rally with lower rates.

STOCK INDUSTRY GROUP

One concept you will frequently encounter as a Teenvestor is industry groupings. An industry represents a business category such as entertainment, real estate, banking, and so on. Investors typically look at companies in the same industry in the same way. For example, if the stock of Chase Manhattan Bank is doing really well, they'd expect other banks to do well also, otherwise they'd suspect something might be wrong with that bank. Industry categories are also important because they can help you decide which businesses are growing and which ones are dying.

Let's take the example of "pinball machines" to emphasize the importance of industry classifications. Before Gameboy, Nintendo, and other electronic games were sold to entertain people with time on their hands, there were pinball machines. Pinball machines were giant, four-legged, box-like machines with metal balls that a player could shoot and score points by directing the balls through a maze. While some adults may still play with pinball machines, young people today require more electronic gadgets for entertainment. An investment in a company that makes only pinball machines would not be ~ise because that segment of the entertainment industry is clearly not ~~ However, if a company that makes pinball machines starts making games that feature the high technology of a Play Station, then maybe it is worth a second look.

The first thing you should consider is whether the industry is growing. Find out whether there are any new products or services the industry is working on that will make it worth your time and money to invest in it.

The Way Investors View How Industries Develop

Investors think of industries as they would of a human being. At first a newborn baby has to be fed and clothed by his parents. This is much like a new industry that needs a lot of money at the beginning before it can even begin to make profits for its investors. In business language this is called the *early development stage*.

The baby starts to walk and feed himself and then quickly grows into a vibrant young child, and then moves through his teenage years. This is much like an industry that is developing quickly and begins selling a lot of its products and services (even though it may still not be making much profit).

The young man marries, starts a family, and watches his children graduate from high school and college. This stage is like an industry that is maturing, attracting a steady stream of customers, and making steady money for its owners. In business language, this is called the *mature or mature growth stage*.

The man eventually begins to feel the aches and pains of old age such as bad knees, a bad back, and other diseases associated with aging bodies. This is like an industry that has fully matured and is in decline. In business language, this is known as the *decline stage*. The pinball machine industry we talked about earlier falls into the declining industry category.

If science develops cures for some of the diseases suffered by the elderly, the man could live a relatively healthy life for a long time. This is like a declining industry that has found ways to keep its products or services fresh. For example, if the pinball company we talked about earlier starts to make hand-held computerized pinball games, such an innovation may extend the life of the company. In business language, this is known as the *stabilization stage*. The decline stage and the stabilization stage go hand in hand because stabilization slows down the decline of an industry.

No one can really tell exactly how long each stage will last or how quickly it take to move from one stage to another. What's important is that you know that companies have their own cycles and you'd want to avoid putting money in declining industries.

ASSIGNMENT 10.1

Make your best guess about the stage of development of each one of the following industries: JC Penney, Yahoo!, and USX. See our website for how to do this assignment if you don't already know.

Why Industry Categories Are Important

Just because you pick a stock you are interested in buying doesn't mean that you can ignore all other stocks in the same indus-
~ver you start researching the stock of a particular company, a list of other companies in the same industry so .e reasonable comparisons. These comparisons are

important because most investors tend to look at companies in the same industry in the same way. For example, they will look at how much revenue and profit companies in the same industry make, how much money they owe, and other comparisons. A good example will be a comparison of the earnings of McDonald's and Wendy's, which are both in the fast food business.

One way to understand the importance of making comparison of companies within industries is to think of runners and the various skills needed for individual events. You wouldn't expect a 100-meter runner to do well in a 10,000-meter (6.2 miles) race because each event requires different skills: the 100-meter runner needs a burst of speed to win his race, while the 10,000 meter runner needs a lot more endurance in order to finish and win his race. It would be impossible to decide who is a better athlete, the sprinter or the long-distance runner, because the events are totally different. You can, however, state that the 100-meter runner is better or worse than other 100-meter runners based on his speed. You *can* say that the 10,000-meter runner is better or worse than other long-distance runners who specialize in the same event. Just as you have to compare athletes in the same events, you have to compare companies in the same industries.

ASSIGNMENT 10.2

Identify the industries of the 30 stocks in the Dow Jones Industrial Average. List three competitors for Dell Computers. See our website for how to complete this assignment if you don't already know.

Difficulties Of Classifying Companies

Sometimes companies make so many types of products that it is hard to tell exactly how to categorize them in terms of industry. The general rule-of-thumb, however, is to put them in categories closest to what they are known for producing.

Fortunately, the Internet is proving to be a useful tool for identifying industry categories of public companies. In fact, some websites such as the ones run by Microsoft Money Central, Multex Investor, and Clearstation, can give you a list of companies in any industry and they can even give you averages for important industry information. Our website, www.teenvestor.com, will point you to the location of good industry information.

ASSIGNMENT 10.3

How would you classify the industry that Pepsico, Seagrams, and USX belong to? Remember to find out the lines of business these companies are in. See our website for how to do this assignment if you don't already know.

BETA - HOW THE RISK OF STOCKS IS MEASURED
(For The Advanced Teenvestor)

The risk of stocks has a special name in the world of finance—*beta*. The simplified explanation of beta is that it tells you how the value of a stock moves up and down with an index like the S&P 500. You don't really have to know how it is calculated but knowing the beta for each stock gives you an idea of how risky it is. If a stock has a beta of 1, it means that its value moves up and down by the same percentage as a market index like the S&P 500 moves up and down. A stock that moves with this index is said to have the same risk as the market. For example, if the S&P 500 index has a value of 5,000 today and moves to 5,500 tomorrow, this represents a 10% increase. If the stock of company XYZ has a beta of 1, you would roughly expect its value to also increase by approximately 10%. A stock like this with a beta of 1 is not really considered risky when compared with the overall stock market. A stock with a beta of, say, 2 means that each time the S&P Index moves up by 10% or so, the stock of company XYZ moves up by 2 x 10% = 20%. It also means that this same stock can move down 20% in value as well. So in general, high beta stocks are riskier than low beta stocks. But some people like risk because, even though they can lose a lot of money, they can also win a lot if the market goes their way.

ASSIGNMENT 10.4

Which one of these companies do you think will have the highest beta: Coca-Cola Company, Sears, Microsoft Corp., and Yahoo!? See our website for how to do this assignment if you don't already know.

DIVERSIFICATION

You have probably heard of the old saying, "don't put all your eggs in one basket." When choosing stocks, investors try to invest in a few different companies so that no one stock that loses its value can affect their whole *portfolio* (the basket of stocks and other investments). The act of investing in several different types of stocks to achieve this goal is called *diversification*.

Investors diversify their portfolios because when a stock goes down or rises in value, other stocks in the same industry tend to go down or rise in value as well. This means that if General Motors stock goes down, the stock of Chrysler is also likely to be lower because the two companies are both in the automobile industry. In order to protect the value of their portfolios, investors diversify by buying the stocks of companies in different industries so as to reduce the chance that the entire portfolio will lose too much value if one industry has a problem. So, for example, an investor might include the following stocks in a portfolio: General Motors (car industry), IBM (computer industry), and McDonald's (food industry). Because these stocks are all in different industries, it is unlikely that a problem in one company will affect the other two companies.

Teenvestors find it hard to diversify because they have very little money to invest with. Nevertheless, it is important to know the value of not putting all your eggs in one basket if you ever get enough cash to spread your investment around to different stocks. If you are forced to invest in just one or two stocks, you then have to make sure that the stocks are as safe as possible.

THE BUSINESS CYCLE

Professional investors on Wall Street and other financial centers around the world view the market as having some type of pattern, which they call the *business cycle*. They observe that businesses (as reflected in the stock market) swing from good times to bad times in a fairly regular manner. There are four major parts of the business cycle: *maturation*, *contraction* (or *recession*), *revival*, and *expansion*.

The economy flows through the four sections of this business cycle and the way this happens is worthy of an explanation.

Let's say that we are at the stage of the business cycle where things are going great. The Dow and the S&P 500 are flying high. (In common business language, when the stock market is booming, investment experts refer to this as a *bull market*). Businesses can't keep up with the demand for their products—they can't supply enough products for consumers. They have to borrow money to invest in more equipment in order to expand their production capabilities. They have to hire more people to make the products and pay them more because they are competing with other companies who also want to hire more people. This stage of the business cycle is known as the maturation stage.

The maturation stage might go on for a long time but at some point, inflation rears its ugly head because more people are employed at higher costs and the costs of materials go up (since companies are buying more and more materials to make their products). This, of course, affects how much profit companies make since their expenses are going up faster than they can increase the price of the items they are selling. Rising inflation (and hence, rising interest rates) sets the groundwork for the next stage of the business cycle—the contraction or recession stage.

In the contraction stage of the business cycle, inflation, and all the bad things it brings, causes businesses to pull back. They pull back also because they have probably overbuilt factories and bought too many machines to make their products in anticipation of continued demand for their products. Given the fact that their profit is going down, they cut back on their equipment purchases, lay off some of the extra workers (especially those hired when things were going great and there was no inflation), cut back on salaries, and take other actions to stop their profits from further declining. With reduced incomes, consumers (or workers) reduce their spending. The stock market indexes enter a downward phase, or a *bear market* as it is commonly called. In this stage of the business cycle, business and consumers do not borrow as much money to buy equipment and other items. The Federal Reserve may even step in to reduce rates (by lowering the discount rate) in order to encourage borrowing and spending.

At some point in the recession and contraction phase, things start to turn around. The stock market, after prices have gone down due to reduced profits, begins to move up again. Recall that rates are low at this point (due to the actions of the Federal Reserve) so people are willing to give up the low rates in bonds to move back into stocks. This sets the stage for the next phase of the business cycle—the revival stage.

In the revival stage of the business cycle, consumers start to feel more confident that the worst is behind them and they start to spend again. Economic indicators like the GDP start to move higher after long periods of decline, employment numbers start to look good again, some businesses start to spend more money again. So after months or years of being in the doldrums, things begin to look good again. This sets the stage for the next stage of the business cycle—the expansion stage.

In the expansion stage of the business cycle, the revival continues and many more businesses benefit from a good economy—not just a few businesses in specific industries. Companies that require heavy investments such as housing construction companies and appliance manufacturers fully benefit from a good economy. The bull market is back again.

The next stage after expansion is the maturation stage. And we are right back where we started with an economy that is in full gear, with The Dow and the S&P 500 making investors very happy.

In truth, it is sometimes difficult to tell whether the economy is in the expansion or in the maturity stage because at some point, the expansion stage moves into the maturity stage (although the Federal Reserve can help a bit to prolong the expansion).

A contraction stage is easier to spot once you are in it. A high unemployment rate and other signs of stress in the economy can give you a clue about when contraction has set in.

Suppose you knew the exact time a stock will hit its lowest level and its highest level in the business cycle. If you knew the exact pattern of a business cycle, you would want to buy the stock when it has hit its lowest level, and sell it when it has hit its highest level (when The Dow and the S&P 500 are at their highest and are just about to come down). As a Teenvestor you can make a fortune if you have the skill to predict the length of the cycles. Unfortunately, no one knows how long each stage of the business cycle will last. In addition, no two business cycles have exactly the same pattern. Therefore, you can't just use a calendar to tell when a new business cycle will begin and end. Some experts say that a 10-year expansion period—the longest expansion in the history of the United States—ended in the latter half of the year 2000. Of course no one knows how long or how far the economy will contract before it starts expanding again.

It is worth mentioning here that the Federal Reserve tries to moderate the good times in the market by raising and lowering the discount rate. However, despite its efforts, business cycles still occur, although not necessarily with the same sting to the economy. The Federal Reserve simply tries to soften the blow when things are bad and, at the same time, makes sure that the good times don't get out of hand (which can cause more inflation). When the Federal Reserve slows an overheated economy down without causing a recession, this is known as a *soft landing*.

EXPECTATIONS VERSUS REALITY

In the previous chapter, we discussed some of the government data that affect the market in one way or another. For example, we talked about how high employment can start inflation because it means that there are more people with money to spend, and this drives prices up. We want to, once again, emphasize why the market sometimes does not behave the way you might expect it to with the announcement of some new economic news. Stock prices are affected when the government's economic data are released to the public only if the numbers people expect the government to publish are different from the numbers it actually publishes. This is very important to understand so we will go through it more slowly here, even though we discussed it in the previous chapter.

At any given point in time, financial experts (and other professional investors) take a guess at the economic numbers that will be published by the government. Some of these experts work in companies such as Merrill Lynch & Co., and J.P. Morgan Chase that spend millions trying to predict what the GDP, inflation (the CPI), the discount rate and employment rates will be the next time the government publishes these numbers. At the same time, other people involved in the market such as stockbrokers, also form their own opinions. Eventually, all these opinions come together and reporters will say things like "analysts say that the unemployment numbers, which will be published by the U.S. Department of Labor next week, will be 4.2% for November" or "Wall Street expects the Federal Reserve to raise the discount rate by 1/2 a percent." Remember that even though these are the opinions of the experts, these opinions can affect the market immediately even before the actual figures are published. When the government publishes the true numbers, a couple of things can happen. If the government's numbers match what the experts predict, the stock market will probably not move very much. If, however, the actual numbers are worse than or better than predicted, the stock market will move in one direction or another. Therefore, the difference between expected economic figures and what the economic figures actually turn out to be is the key to the changing fortunes of the stock market. To drive the point home, in a front page story in *The London Financial Times* titled "Fed Increases Rates to 5.75% Amid Fears Over The Spread Of Expansion," the writer said the following:

> Financial markets were little moved by the
> widely expected decision (to raise rates).

Here, the newspaper is saying that the market already assumed that the rate rise was going to happen anyway so stock prices had already adjusted (in anticipation of a rate hike) before the Federal Reserve raised rates. When the Federal Reserve Bank finally increased rates, nothing happened to the stock market because the market had already adjusted before the rate hike. So, you can see that what we have been telling you actually happens in real life.

THE VARIOUS STOCK CLASSIFICATIONS

Investors love to put stocks into various categories in order to make it easier to identify them. There are probably over one dozen stock classifications but we will describe only the following five here: *blue-chip*, *growth*, *income*, *cyclical*, and *interest-rate-sensitive* stocks.

Blue-chip stocks are stocks of the biggest companies in the country. They are usually the stocks of high quality companies with years of strong profit and steady dividend payments. They are also some of the safest stocks to invest in. You will probably not get rich overnight by investing in these stocks but you will sleep better knowing that you won't lose your hard-earned money either. The stocks that are part of The Dow, for example, are considered blue-chip stocks.

Growth stocks are stocks of companies with profits that are increasing quickly. This increase in profits is reflected in the rise in the company's stock price. The definition of the level of profit growth that determines whether a stock is a growth stock varies from time to time. At the present time, however, a net profit growth of 15% to 20% is the standard. Just as a tree can't grow to the heavens, a stock can't grow forever. At some point, the growth rate will slow down to modest growth of 10% or less.

A growth company usually spends a lot of money on research and puts all its profits back into the company instead of paying dividends. In addition, it usually sells unique products and, these days, it is likely to be a high technology company that depends on intellectual power (such as software companies). Some software, Internet, and other computer-related companies can be considered growth companies. While the stock prices of growth companies increase at a more rapid rate than the stocks of some blue-chip companies, they are also riskier because their prices can tumble just as quickly as they rise.

Income stocks are the stocks of stable companies that pay large dividends. Older people who are retired often buy stocks in these stable income companies since it provides them with a steady income—more than they can earn by investing in bonds or putting their money in savings accounts. These investors are more interested in getting cash in their hands to meet their modest lifestyles than in investing in the more risky growth stocks, which are more risky. Institutions such as colleges also put their money in income stocks to provide them with a steady stream of dividends to keep their doors open instead of depending on stock prices to go up. The stocks of electric utility companies are typically considered income stocks.

Cyclical stocks are stocks in companies whose fortunes go up and down with the business cycle. Stock prices of these companies go up when general business conditions are good (as reflected by a bull market) and the prices go down when general business conditions are bad (such as in a bear market). Cyclical companies usually invest in heavy equipment to make their products and they are known for laying people off when business is down. Cyclical companies can be found in the following types of industries: paper, chemicals, steel, machinery and machine tools, airlines, railroads and railroad equipment, and automobiles.

Interest-rate sensitive stocks are stocks that are affected primarily by changes in interest rates. Banks and other financial companies can be considered interest-rate sensitive companies. These companies feel the effects of any move by the Federal Reserve to hold off inflation or to kick-start the economy.

STOCK INVESTMENT APPROACHES

Investors have two major classifications for their investment methods: *growth* investing and *value* investing. Most people use investment strategies that combine both growth and value investing.

Growth investors look for stocks of companies whose sales and earning are growing rapidly each year—perhaps a growth of 15-20% or more each year. Oftentimes they look for stock prices that are shooting up—that is, they look for *momentum* (otherwise known as forward movement) in these stocks. The stock prices may be high compared to the earnings of the companies, but growth investors don't care. Growth investors also have the tendency to trade a lot of shares in and out of their portfolio. They keep an eye on their stock prices and sell their shares as soon as they see that the growth of the companies in which they have invested has slowed down.

Value investors sometimes look for stocks that have fallen on hard times, and therefore are relatively cheap compared with their prior prices. They also look for stocks that have been overlooked by other investors for one reason or another. In other words, they are looking for a bargain and hoping to buy shares before prices go up (when more people realize that the stock is a bargain).

RETURN ON INVESTMENT

On of the most basic financial concepts is the *return on investment*, also known as *return*. Return on investment measures how

much profit you have gained or lost (in percentage terms) by investing in stocks, mutual funds, bonds, a business venture, a bank account, or any other type of financial product. When you put your
money in a bank account that pays interest, you are making a loan to
the bank for which you get a small profit—the interest. Your investment is the loan to the bank and the return on your investment is the
interest rate paid by the bank.

The return on investment for a stock is not guaranteed, as is the
case with a bank deposit. For stocks, the return on investment depends on how much stock prices increase after you've bought your
shares. In general, the before-tax return of a stock and other investments, which are held for a one-year period, can be calculated as follows:

ROI = [(End Value - Beginning Value) / (Beginning Value)] x 100

Where End Value is the price received for selling the investment.

Where Beginning Value is the price you paid when you purchased the investment. (We assume there are no fees charged by anyone who helped you buy
or sell the investment).

So if you bought a share of stock for $50 and sold it one year
later for $60, your return can be calculated as follows:

ROI = [($60-$50) / ($50)] x 100 = [($10) / ($50)] x 100 = 20% per year

Return on investment gets slightly more complicated if you
hold the investment for less than one year or for over one year. We
will spare you the agony of the mathematics here—you can learn
more about it on www.teenvestor.com.

COMPOUNDING (For The Advanced Teenvestor)

Compounding refers to the rate at which money grows if you automatically reinvest all the profit you make in the same investment. To help you understand the concept of compounding, we will use a simple example of a bank account that pays interest. A bank can pay you two kinds of interest: simple interest or compound interest. Suppose you have $1,000 in the bank that pays 10% simple interest per year for 10 years. Each year, you will earn $100 interest on your $1,000 investment (in the bank account) as calculated below:

Yearly Interest = Yearly Interest Percentage x Deposit Amount

Yearly Interest = 10% x $1,000 = .1 x $1,000 = $100

The yearly simple interest for the 10-year period is shown below:

	Simple Interest		Principal Balance		Interest Earned on Principal
1.	10%	x	$1,000.00	=	$100.00
2.	10%	x	$1,000.00	=	$100.00
3.	10%	x	$1,000.00	=	$100.00
4.	10%	x	$1,000.00	=	$100.00
5.	10%	x	$1,000.00	=	$100.00
6.	10%	x	$1,000.00	=	$100.00
7.	10%	x	$1,000.00	=	$100.00
8.	10%	x	$1,000.00	=	$100.00
9.	10%	x	$1,000.00	=	$100.00
10.	10%	x	$1,000.00	=	$100.00
					$1,000.00

As you can see, the total amount of simple interest earned in the 10-year period is $1,000. We calculated this amount by multiplying the yearly interest of 10% by the initial amount you deposited in your account (the *principal balance* of $1,000) and adding up the resulting products for the 10-year period. Since you get back your initial principal balance of $1,000, you will receive a total of $2,000 at the end of the

10-year period. Remember that this simple interest method shown in the example above assumes that your yearly profit of $100 is not reinvested into the account.

If the bank tells you that you will earn 10% yearly compound interest on your deposit (instead of 10% simple interest), you will make more on your investment than in the simple interest case. Once again, on a yearly basis, you will be earning 10% profit on your principal. But the difference in this case is that your yearly profit (i.e. your yearly interest) will be reinvested each year into the bank account, and not taken out, as was the case with the simple interest calculation above. Here is how your money will stack up each year with compound interest:

	Compound Interest		Principal Balance		Interest Earned on Principal
1.	10%	x	$1,000.00	=	$100.00
2.	10%	x	$1,100.00	=	$110.00
3.	10%	x	$1,210.00	=	$121.00
4.	10%	x	$1,331.00	=	$133.10
5.	10%	x	$1,464.00	=	$146.40
6.	10%	x	$1,610.50	=	$161.05
7.	10%	x	$1,771.60	=	$177.16
8.	10%	x	$1,948.70	=	$194.87
9.	10%	x	$2,143.60	=	$214.36
10.	10%	x	$2,357.90	=	$235.79
					$1,593.73

With yearly compounding, the interest earned in one year is reinvested into the bank account in the next year. You can tell that this is the case because the Principal Balance column above is increasing so interest is applied to a bigger and bigger principal balance each year. With the yearly compound interest method, the principal balance increases from $1,000 in the first year to $2,357.90 in the tenth year. With the simple interest method, the principal balance stays at $1,000 for all ten years. At the end of the tenth year for the yearly compound interest example, the total interest earned is $1,593.73 as opposed to $1,000 with simple interest—a difference of $593.73.

Compounding can be done yearly (as is the case in our example), monthly, daily, or in any other time interval. Once again, we will spare you the agony of the mathematics here but we can show you how it is done on www.teenvestor.com if you are curious.

In our prior two examples, the total compound interest was higher than the total simple interest by $593.73. This may seem like a small number, but remember that we assumed you deposited only $1,000 for a 10-year period. As the initial deposit balance increases, the difference between compounding interest and simple interest gets bigger and bigger. As the time the money stays in the account (or in the investment) increases, this difference also gets bigger and bigger.

The reason we are telling you all of this is because compounding also has a big effect on the money you put into stocks, bonds, mutual funds, and other investments. We will now apply this concept to the return on investment in stocks.

Recall that in our introduction, we mentioned that over the past 72 years, the average return on investment for stocks was about 11% per year. This means that on the average, someone investing in stocks (and reinvesting all her dividends as well) could have made 11% profit each year over a long, long period of time. Because of the compounding effect of investments, a long-term investor can double her money every seven or eight years if we assume an 11% annual profit. Imagine the profit if the investment balance were bigger. This multiplication effect of invested money is one of the reasons it is wise to invest for the long run. We will explain more about this concept at a later chapter.

The power of compounding is so important to investors that a formula called *the rule of 72* has been devised to tell any investor about how much time it will take to double her money given a yearly compound rate. The rule of 72 states that if you divide 72 by an assumed compound rate, you would get the approximate number of years it will take to double your money. The formula is as follows:

Time To Double Your Money = 72 / Interest Rate

So, if the compound rate is 11%, the formula is as follows:

Time To Double Your Money = 72 / 11 = 6.55 years

Thus, the approximate time to double your money at a compound rate of 11% per year is 6.55 years (or about 7 years). At a compound rate of 22% per year, it will take about 3.27 years (72 / 22 = 3.27 years).

THE TIME VALUE OF MONEY
(For The Advanced Teenvestor)

The *time value of money* is another very important investing concept. The application of this idea is what determines your parents' monthly mortgage, car loan payment, or installment loan payments. It also has an effect on the price of stocks.

Time value of money simply says that a dollar received today is worth more than a dollar received in one day, one month, or a year because the dollar received today can start earning interest immediately. It is such a simple idea that you probably already know it, but you just haven't thought about how it can affect your actions. Let's consider an example of how this idea can be applied.

Suppose someone told you that you can have $100,000 today or you can have $105,000 a year from now (assuming you have no immediate need for the money). Which would you prefer?

You cannot really answer this question until we supply you with one more piece of information: the return you can earn in one year by putting the $100,000 in an alternate investment. You can easily answer the question if you know that you can put the $100,000 you'd receive today, in a bank account paying 10% yearly compound interest.

Think about the choices again: receive $100,000 today or receive $105,000 one year from now. For those of you who would rather have the $105,000 one year from now, you would have cheated yourself out of $5,000. If you collect $100,000 today, you can deposit it in the bank and earn 10% interest for the year, or $10,000, on that money. In one year, you would have a principal and interest total of $110,000. This is $5,000 more than you would get if you'd opted to receive $105,000 one year in the future.

If we told you that you can have $100,000 today or $110,000 one year from now, both choices are equivalent because the extra $10,000 we would give you one year from now exactly equals the amount of money you can earn by investing $100,000 in the bank for one year.

This time value of money idea means that if you have a choice of receiving money today or a year from now, the money you should expect a year from now should be higher than the money you are offered today.

Turning the situation around a bit, suppose someone told you that you are eligible to receive $100,000 one year from now. At the same time, she asks you how much money you'd require today such that you'd give up the $100,000 money you can receive in a year? Once again, this will depend on how much you can earn by investing the money you would get today for one year. Let's go through the numbers.

Assume again that the interest rate you can get by putting your money in a bank is 10% yearly compound rate. The question you have to ask yourself is this: how much will I have to put in a bank account which pays 10% yearly compound interest such that at the end of one year I'd have $100,000? Mathematically, the equation to solve is as follows:

Future Value = (Present Value) + (Present Value) x (Rate On Investment)

Where Future Value is the amount of money you would get in the future, which is $100,000 in our example.

Where Present Value is the amount of money you would need today such that if you invested it in a bank today, you would end up with the Future Balance.

Where Rate On Investment is the interest rate you would be paid for your investment, which is 10% in our example.

What we are trying to figure out in the equation above is Present Value—how much you would need today such that if you invest it, you would end up with $100,000 in a year. We can easily solve the equation as follows:

Future Value = (Present Value) + (Present Value) x (Rate On Investment)

With a bit of manipulation, we get the following formula:

Future Value = (Present Value) x (1 + Rate On Investment)

With more manipulation, we get the following formula:

Present Value = Future Value / (1 + Rate On Investment)

Substituting the numbers in our example, we get the following equation:

Present Value = $100,000 / (1 + 10%) = $100,000 / (1 + .1) = $100,000 / 1.1
Present Value = $90,909.09

Remember the original question: how much cash would you require today such that you would not have to be paid $100,000 one year from now? As you can see from the formula above, the answer is that you should require at least $90,909.09 today, and we can prove it. With $90,909.09 on hand today, you could put it in a bank account earning 10% per year. The total amount of money you would have in one year if you invest this money in the bank (Future Value) would be calculated as follows:

Future Value = $90,909.09 + ($90,909.09) x (10%)
Future Value = $90,909.09 + $9090.909 = $100,000

If we changed the original question and asked how much cash you would require today such that you would not have to be paid $100,000 two years from now, the answer gets slightly more complicated but the basic principle is the same. You just need to know how much money you would need today such that if you earn 10% interest in the first year, and earn another 10% interest in the second year, you would end up with $100,000. Without going through the mathematics, the answer is $82,644.63. We can prove it as follows:

Year#1 Future Value = $82,644.63 + ($82,644.63) x (10%) = $90,909.09

The investment balance for the second year's investment is now $90,909.09 so at the end of the second year, you would end up with:

Year#2 Future Value = $90,909.09 + ($90,909.09) x (10%) = $100,000

So as you can see, you should require $82,644.63 today such that you would give up $100,000 two years from now. Notice that we have quietly used the compounding concept here because we assumed that in the second year, the new invested balance includes the interest earned in the first year.

The terms *present value* and *future value* have very special meanings in the investment world. Present value refers to today's value of a sum of money to be received in the future. If someone asks you for the present value of $100,000, you would need two pieces of additional information from them: how far in the future the money will be received and the rate of investment [or *discount rate* (not to be confused with the Federal Reserve Bank's discount rate in Chapter 9), as it is commonly known in finance lingo when calculating present value] that is to be applied. In our example, the present value of $100,000 to be received in two years, and to which a discount rate of 10% is applied was $82,644.63. Though we didn't show you the calculation for this, the present value of $100,000 to be received in fifty years and to which a 10% discount rate is to be applied is $852.86. That's correct—if someone gave you $852.86 today, you would get $100,000 back in 50 years if the interest rate or discount rate were assumed to be 10%.

Future value is easier to understand because you are already used to calculating it whether you know it or not. Future value is how much you would earn by making an investment today and collecting your money in the future. Like present value, you will need to know the rate of investment and the amount of time in which you will receive the cash. When calculating future value, however, the rate of investment is known as the *investment rate*—the percentage return (analogous to the interest in our bank deposit example). So, the future value of $82,644.63 in two years assuming a 10% compound investment rate is $100,000 (as we calculated earlier). Though we didn't show you the calculation for this, the future value of $100,000 to be received in fifty years and to which a 10% compound investment rate is to be applied is $11,739,085.

HOW THE TIME VALUE OF MONEY AND STOCK PRICES ARE RELATED (For The Advanced Teenvestor)

In Chapter 9, we briefly mentioned how inflation affects the stock market, but we didn't really give you a full explanation. We can now give you the details here because we've covered the meaning of present value.

In general, stock prices depend on how much investors expect companies to make in the future. You can think of the change in the price of a stock as the result of a vote by investors on whether they think the company will make more or less money in the future. If more investors think the company will do better in the future than those who think the company will do worse in the future, the price of a stock will go up because of the law of supply and demand as discussed earlier in the chapter. Likewise, if more investors think the company will do worse in the future than those who think the company will do better in the future, the price of a stock will go down.

When you add the element of inflation, the movement in the price of stock gets more interesting. The higher the inflation rate, the smaller the present value of a company's future earnings because inflation increases the discount rate to be applied to future earnings of the company. If you recall our previous discussion, the present value of money to be received in the future is as follows:

Present Value = Future Value / (1 + Rate On Investment)
Where Rate On Investment is the discount rate

As the denominator of the equation above increases (that is, as the discount rate increases), the present value of the company's future earnings gets smaller and smaller. What this means is that a company's future earnings is worth less and less as inflation creeps up because inflation is reflected in the discount rate—the higher the inflation, the higher the discount rate. This is the main reason why investors hate inflation.

Our website, www.teenvestor.com, contains more information on business and financial concepts you should know.

11

HOW TO FIND THE RIGHT STOCK

There are probably over 10,000 stocks you can buy for your investment portfolio. There is no way you can investigate each one of these stocks to see which ones are likely to increase in value. Our general investment advice to Teenvestors is that they should invest in what they know *and* in products in which they have an interest—at least at the beginning of their life-long investment efforts. The important thing is to get started buying the stocks of strong companies that will be around for a long time.

It is important that you make a habit of investing in stocks on a periodic basis. Once a month, two times a year—it doesn't matter as long as you make it a priority to put your money in stocks that are likely to grow. We have a few suggestions that can help you decide what stocks to buy.

THE BUSINESSES IN WHICH YOUR RELATIVES WORK

Unless your parents work for the government, you can get good investment ideas by talking to them about the companies and the industries in which they work to see if these companies are good investment opportunities. They can tell you whether there are innovative things their companies are doing that will make for attractive investments. For example, we bought a car from a dealer through the Internet by using an online company called Autobytel. The salesperson at the dealership where we picked up the car told us that he was getting more and more car orders through the Internet. As it turned out, shortly after our purchase, Autobytel went public (that is, it started selling stock to the public). Had the salesperson been someone we know on a social basis, he may have been able to alert us to the trends in his industry regarding online auto sales. We would have been on the lookout for companies like Autobytel that enable consumers to shop for cars online. Not that we would have purchased the company's stock, especially given the downturn in Internet stocks, but we would have at least paid more attention to the profitability of Internet automobile transactions.

Ask your parents to bring back any annual reports or brochures the company produces for the public. Your parents can give you some insight on the trends in the industry, the competitors, and the general feelings of the employees in the company. Keep in mind, however, that there is a limit to the amount of information your parents are allowed to pass on to you. This is because senior managers at companies can't benefit from certain information they know about their companies (called *insider information*) unless the information has been released to the general public.

Don't just stop with your parents. Your other relatives and neighbors have a wealth of knowledge you can tap to learn about what is going on in different industries. They can alert you to trends before everyone else knows about them. Make a habit of asking about the businesses they are in and about any exciting products or services their companies are developing. Once again, you can ask these relatives for annual reports and other publicly available information that may help you understand the industry in which they work.

Speaking of friends and relatives, you should do your own research before making any purchases. Some people have a habit of boasting about their great investments without mentioning their losses in the market. There are no sure things when it comes to investing in the stock market.

CONSIDER YOUR HOBBIES

Hobbies are often a good place to start when looking for investment opportunities. If your hobby is collectibles, for example, you may be interested in learning more about companies that specialize in sports memorabilia, art, toys, and other collectibles for hobbyists. You can probably find a stock associated with any kind of hobby you can think of. If you like in-line skating, you can find a company that makes the equipment, the pads, and other items associated with the activity. If you like sports, there are some publicly traded companies such as The Boston Celtics.

To recap, our philosophy is that when you first begin investing, follow your interests. When you become an experienced Teenvestor, you can then move on to investments that look promising—whether you have a passion for those businesses or not.

LOOK TO YOUR FRIENDS AND CLASSMATES FOR IDEAS

Other young people are excellent sources of good investment ideas. Just by observation of what your friends and classmates love to wear and eat, you can see some good investment potential. The entertainment they choose and the beverages they drink can also be a clue to the right stocks. For example, if you notice that your classmates prefer Powerade instead of Gatorade, perhaps this is a sign that you should look at investing in Powerade. Look around your school for items that are popular among your classmates. Look around your house for products, foods, and gadgets that your family prefers. Ideas are everywhere. Don't limit yourself to just what is in your immediate environment. The only things to watch out for are items that are too trendy because they will probably fade away in a year or two.

START READING BUSINESS PUBLICATIONS

Teenvestors should read business magazines and newspapers available in the market. Fortunately, 13-year olds can read and understand most general business publications. We even know an 11-year old who reads *The Wall Street Journal* on a regular basis.

In our opinion, *The Wall Street Journal* should be required reading for every Teenvestor. Find a copy and, at the very least, just stare at the front page—you are sure to absorb something from this great publication. In addition, high-quality business magazines such as *Forbes*, *Fortune*, and *Business Week* sometimes do long articles on big companies. These publications can often save Teenvestors lots of research time because they publish detailed up-to-date articles on some of the biggest companies in the United States. The important business magazines can be found in most libraries, in newspaper stands and on the Internet.

There are also some relatively new magazines such as *Business 2.0*, *Industry Standard*, and *Fast Company*, which write about technology companies. Although we feel that high technology investing is for the advanced Teenvestor, you may want to sample some of these magazines as well (if they are still in existence given the wipeout of Internet companies in the past two years). Here is a list of the publications that will help you become a true Teenvestor:

> The Wall Street Journal
> Investor's Business Daily
> Business Week
> Fortune
> Forbes
> Individual Investor
> Business 2.0
> Kiplinger's
> Mutual Funds
> Money
> Black Enterprise
> Hispanic Business
> Fast Company
> Smart Money
> Family Money
> Industry Standard

If your parents have a subscription to *The Wall Street Journal*, you can get an online version of the paper at a discounted rate. (See www.teenvestor.com for links to these publications.)

LOOK AT THE COMPANIES HEADQUARTERED IN YOUR STATE

If you look around, you will notice that there are some big companies with headquarters in your state. This is probably no surprise to you if you live in the eastern states such as New York, New

Jersey or Massachusetts. But states with smaller populations also have sizeable corporations. Because these companies are in your state (or in some cases, in your city), you may be able to get information from them more quickly. In addition, your family may even know people who work for them who can help you in deciding whether they are good candidates for your investment dollar. The annual *Fortune 500* edition of *Fortune* magazine usually lists the biggest companies in the U.S. by geographical areas. Look for a copy in your local library or purchase one from your local newsstand.

TRY CHOOSING SPECIFIC INDUSTRIES

Another way to determine which companies are worth investing in is to identify an *industry* category that interests you. An industry category defines the line of business a company is in. For example, Walt Disney is in the entertainment industry while Dell Computers is in the computer industry. This technique is useful if, through your research and reading of business publications, you determine that a particular industry will be a good investment but you don't know exactly which companies in that industry will make for the best investment. Knowing the industry of the company in which you want to invest also makes it easier for you to compare how the company is doing relative to other companies in the same line of business. Table 11.1, on the next page, gives a list of some of the industry categories used by investors. This list was created by Multex Investor, which runs one of our favorite research websites, www.multexinvestor.com. Many other organizations, such as Standard & Poor's and Moody's, have their own industry categories although the major categories from one company to another are quite similar.

TABLE 11.1
Industry Categories (by Multex Investor)

Advertising	Fabricated Plastic &	Oil Well Services &
Aerospace & Defense	Rubber	Equipment
Air Courier	Fish/Livestock	Paper & Paper
Airline	Food Processing	Products
Apparel/Accessories	Footwear	Personal &
Appliance & Tool	Forestry & Wood	Household Prods.
Audio & Video Equip.	Products	Personal Services
Auto & Truck	Furniture & Fixtures	Photography
Manufacturers	Gold & Silver	Printing & Publishing
Auto & Truck Parts	Healthcare Facilities	Printing Services
Beverages (Alcoholic)	Hotels & Motels	Railroads
Beverages (Non-Alc.)	Insurance (Accident	Real Estate Operations
Biotechnology & Drugs	& Health)	Recreational Activities
Broadcasting & Cable	Insurance (Life)	Recreational Products
Business Services	Insurance	Regional Banks
Casinos & Gaming	(Miscellaneous)	Rental & Leasing
Chemical Manufact.	Insurance (Prop. &	Restaurants
Chemicals - Plastics &	Casualty)	Retail (Apparel)
Rubber	Investment Services	Retail (Catalog & Mail
Coal	Iron & Steel	Order)
Communications	Jewelry &	Retail (Department &
Equipment	Silverware	Discount)
Communications Svc.	Major Drugs	Retail (Drugs)
Computer Hardware	Medical Equipment	Retail (Grocery)
Computer Networks	& Supplies	Retail (Home
Computer Peripherals	Metal Mining	Improvement)
Computer Services	Misc. Capital Goods	Retail (Specialty)
Computer Storage	Misc. Fabricated	Retail (Technology)
Devices	Products	S&Ls/Savings Banks
Conglomerates	Misc. Financial	Schools
Constr. & Agric.	Services	Scientific & Technical
Machinery	Misc. Transportation	Instr.
Constr. - Supplies &	Mobile Homes	Security Systems &
Fixtures	& RVs	Services
Construction - Raw	Money Center	Semiconductors
Materials	Banks	Software & Programming
Construction Services	Motion Pictures	Textiles - Non Apparel
Consumer Financial	Natural Gas Utilities	Tires
Services	Non-Metallic Mining	Tobacco
Containers &	Office Equipment	Trucking
Packaging	Office Supplies	Waste Management
Crops	Oil & Gas –	Services
Electric Utilities	Integrated	Water Transportation
Electronic	Oil & Gas	Water Utilities
Instr. & Controls	Operations	

AVOID CHAT ROOM IDEAS

There are lots of online chat groups that discuss investments. Some people probably get good investment ideas from these chat groups. However, you should know that some of the chatters have been known to be individuals who benefit economically from the companies they are chatting about. By making these companies sound like real bargains, they lure unsuspecting investors into investing in them while they dump their own stocks in the market.

In 2000, 15-year-old Jonathan Lebed became the youngest person ever charged with violating Securities and Exchange Commission (SEC) regulations. The SEC, the law enforcement organization for the financial markets, accused Jonathan of involvement in a "pump and dump" scheme. The organization claimed that Jonathan posted messages in chat rooms touting stocks of very tiny companies that he happened to have invested in. As people who believed him bought the stocks, he quietly sold (i.e. dumped) the shares he owned because they were worth more after he pumped up their value on the Internet. According to the SEC, Jonathan made over $800,000 with this scheme. Jonathan settled the case with the SEC without admitting or denying guilt but the case illustrates how people can be fooled into buying stock by listening to chat room "experts."

If you need another reasons not to chat your way into investing, how about two words: *insider trading*. Insider trading is when you use important information that is not public (that is, the company has not released the information to the general public) to make money. In 2000, the U.S. government, for the first time, charged a bunch of people who met each other in a chat room, with sharing insider information on the Internet. One man passed information to another, and another, and it mushroomed from there. Everyone who got information and bought stock based on that information, whether the information was from the initial source or not, was held responsible by the government.

BE SCEPTICAL OF WALL STREET STOCK ANALYSTS

Each major Wall Street financial institution (such as Merrill Lynch, Goldman Sachs, J.P. Morgan Chase, etc.), has analysts that give their opinions on industries and on specific companies. At the same time, each of these financial institutions has investment bankers that solicit business from those same industries and companies covered by analysts. It should go without saying that analysts' opinions about the financial health of the companies that they analyze should not be influenced by the amount of business their investment banking colleagues solicit from these same companies. But this does not always happen. Analysts have been known to give glowing comments about companies that do business with investment banking colleagues. Here's how *The Wall Street Journal,* on July 11, 2001, described the problem:

> For years, some analysts at Wall Street's most prominent firms have compromised their work, caving into pressure from investment bankers at the firms—who believe negative research will harm the chances of winning corporate-finance deals—or from angry corporate clients or portfolio managers. At the same time, analysts themselves often owned shares in the companies they covered.

Since the crash of Internet stocks in 2000 and the down turn in the stock market through 2001, Wall Street analysts have come under increased scrutiny by the government and investors alike. In 2001, the SEC, Congress, and state regulators began to carefully examine the objectivity of these analysts. In addition, more investors are suing companies for what they believe is biased investment advice. Merrill Lynch, for example, is being sued by an investor because he claims he bought stock in a company called Infospace, Inc. on the "buy" recommendation of Merrill's star technology analyst, Henry Blodget. The investor maintains that the reason Mr. Blodget recommended Infospace stock was that Merrill Lynch's investment banking arm was hoping for a deal with Infospace. Merrill Lynch denies the allegation but you can see the type of suspicions that can be raised about the truthfulness of analysts.

What does this mean for you as a Teenvestor? It means that you shouldn't believe "all the hype" by analysts without doing your own research. Just because you see a well-dressed, charismatic analyst on CNBC doesn't mean that his advice is not biased. He may own shares in the company he is raving about or his company may be doing other business with the company.

ASSIGNMENT 11.1

Match each company to an industry. Our site, www.teenvestor.com, will provide links to these companies' websites if you can't figure it out.

Company	Industry
Chase Manhattan Bank	Advertising
Coca-Cola	Air Courier
Continental Air	Hotels & Motels
Exxon Mobil	Apparel/Accessories
Federal Express	Beverages
Gateway 2000	Chemicals
Goodyear	Computers & Peripherals
J.C. Penney	Computer Networks
Marriott International	Airline
Merck & Co.	Retail (Drugs)
Microsoft	Major Drugs
Monsanto	Money Center Banks
Oglivy & Mather	Oil & Gas
CVS	Insurance
Prudential	Software & Services
Yahoo!	Tires

ASSIGNMENT 11.2

Make a list of 10 items and products you encounter or see on a daily basis, which you think might make good investments. Think of items in your home or school, recreational activities such as sports arcades, amusement parks, etc.

	ITEM	COMPANY	INDUSTRY
1			
2			
3			
4			
5			
6			
7			
8			
9			
10			

Our website, www.teenvestor.com, contains more information on how to find the right stocks.

12

EVALUATING STOCKS: UNDERSTANDING WHAT COMPANIES DO

There are two approaches investors use in evaluating stocks: *fundamental analysis* and *technical analysis*. Fundamental stock analysts focus on a company's ability to grow and make more money in the future. They do so by looking at: how much money the company has made in the past, how much money it has borrowed, how much dividend it has paid out to investors, how good its managers are, and other things that may affect the long-term profitability of the company. In considering how good a company's managers are, a fundamental analyst might look at the qualifications of a new Chief Executive Officer (CEO). If the new CEO is coming from another company that he whipped into shape and made more profitable, this is great news for the fundamental analyst. The fundamental analyst would be optimistic that this CEO will do wonders for his new company.

Unlike fundamental analysts, technical analysts focus on how stock prices move up and down and how many shares of a company's stock are bought and sold on a day-to-day basis. Pure technical analysts don't usually concern themselves with the company's historical earnings or how wonderful the management may be. They are more likely to chart the up and down movements of a company's stock price for a period of time. By looking at the pattern of such movements, good technical analysts can sometimes predict which direction stock prices will move. The truth of the matter is that there are probably no pure fundamental or technical analysts. Fundamental analysts often apply some technical analysis, and vice versa. In this chapter, we will teach you the first rule of basic fundamental analysis: understanding what a company does.

GETTING AN OVERVIEW OF THE COMPANY

Knowledge of what a company does and the various kinds of businesses it is in is perhaps the most important item to understand when you first begin your evaluation of a company. In addition, you should identify other companies that may be in the same business as the company you are investigating; this way, you can make comparisons between this company and its competitors.

The Company's Stock Symbol

Each company has a stock symbol used for identification. This symbol makes it easier to list the stock on exchanges such as the New York Stock Exchange and the NASDAQ, where stocks are bought and sold. Before you can find the proper stock symbol for a company, you need to know the company's proper name. Because some companies have their names boldly written on the items they sell, you can easily identify the products they make. For example, you can guess that Nike shoes are made by Nike. However, the names of some products are not necessarily the names of the companies that make them. For example, the snack food Doritos is made by Frito-Lay, which is owned by PepsiCo, Inc.—the same company that makes Pepsi-Cola, Mountain Dew, Slice, and Tropicana. If the product is easily available such as candy or potato chips, you can usually find the name of the company on the container or wrapper.

If you have no clue about who makes a particular product (or delivers a particular service), you can always do a search of the product on the Internet using one of the search engines like Northern Light, Google, or Yahoo!. The result of your search should produce the name of the companies that make the products in which you are interested in investing. If you use the search functions in the sites of financial publications, you may even find the stock symbols of these companies because they are often included in financial articles.

Once you have the proper name of the company that you are interested in investing in, you need to know the stock symbol in order to get more information about the company. These days, nearly all investment sites will give you a company's stock symbol if you type in that company's name or part of its name.

When you type in a stock symbol in the various financial websites, you will see the latest financial information about the company.

The first information that you are likely to see after typing in a stock symbol in a financial website is the latest stock price, along with the change in price from the previous day. You will notice that stock prices are shown in mixed number format—that is, in whole numbers and fractions such as $50^{1/8}$, $34^{1/2}$, $34^{31/32}$, and $34^{31/32}$. The fractions represent fractions of a dollar. For example, the fraction 1/8 is $1/8^{th}$ of a dollar or .125 times a dollar, which is equal to12.5 cents since a dollar is 100 cents. So, the stock price of $50^{1/8}$ can be interpreted as $50 and 12.5 cents, or $50.125. The various exchanges (the NYSE, AMEX, NASDAQ, and others) will soon begin to show stock prices in decimal format instead of in mixed numbers. So instead of seeing a price like $34^{1/2}$, you will see 34.50 in newspaper *stock tables* (which list the prices of each major stock traded on exchanges).

Speaking of stock tables, you will find that there is no need to learn how to read newspaper stock tables since you can easily get stock prices from the Internet. If you would like to learn how to read the stock tables found in newspapers anyway, that information is on our site, www.teenvestor.com.

ASSIGNMENT 12.1

On our website, www.teenvestor.com, you will find instructions on how to get the stock symbol of any public company, and accompanying links to help you do just that. Find the stock symbols of the following companies: Yahoo!, PepsiCo Inc., Tommy Hilfiger Inc., Nike, and Microsoft Corporation. In addition, find the stock symbols of the companies that own Juicy Fruit gum and MTV, the music television station.

The Annual Report

Once you know the company you want to invest in, you should write or call the company for an *annual report*. Annual reports are usually magazine-size booklets that public companies send out yearly to their stockholders, the media, and potential investors to tell the world how the companies are doing. They are produced a few months after the end of a company's fiscal year. Annual reports are usually written to make the companies look really good but the Security and Exchange Commission (SEC) requires that they provide some standard financial information.

Although you can get most of the information about any company through the Internet, we think you should have a real copy of the annual report of the company you are evaluating so you can have a handy reference for your research. In addition, the annual report is your best source for timely and accurate information because some financial websites don't update company information as regularly as they should. You can typically write or call the *investor relations* department of any big company for its annual report.

ASSIGNMENT 12.2

Call the investor relations phone number of one or two companies and ask for their annual reports.

Basic Description Of The Company's Operation

The annual report will take some time before it arrives in the mail, so in the meantime you have to continue your research about the stock of the company in which you want to invest.

Big companies like Ford, Coca-Cola, and J.P. Morgan Chase have traditionally provided investors with lots of information about their operations. But as for the smaller and less widely known businesses, it used to be much harder to get an idea of the products or services they provide without spending lots of time in the library. Fortunately, the Internet has made gathering information about companies a lot easier.

You would think that what a company does is pretty obvious. But in some cases, it is hard to know exactly what a company does until you do more research. Take a company like the General Electric Company (GE), for example. Most people will tell you that GE makes appliances such as refrigerators, microwave ovens, and so on. Some may even be able to tell you that GE also operates television stations and that it owns the NBC television network. But did you know that the company also makes aircraft engines? Don't assume you know what a company does until you do your research.

Sometimes a company can be in so many different businesses that it is hard to pinpoint what it does. We tell Teenvestors to avoid companies that go into various businesses that are not related in one way or another. For example, if Coca-Cola decided to go into the furniture business, this would be a sure sign that the company has lost its focus.

Websites where you can do your company research have write-ups called *snapshots*, or *capsules* (or other names that give you the idea that the descriptions are summaries about the activities of public companies). You can find these summaries in most good financial sites. However, you will start to notice one thing about a lot of snapshots—many of them look the same. The reason is that companies that run financial websites often buy their snapshots from just a handful of companies. One company, Hoover's, provides snapshots for some prominent financial websites. We like Hoover's because the company has a witty writing style and it provides snapshots on even very tiny public companies.

Keep in mind that a snapshot is just the starting point for finding out what a company does. There are lots of articles in the business publications and the newspapers we mentioned in Chapter 11 that can provide you with the information you need to make intelligent decisions about investing. Many of these publications are online and you can access them through our website.

ASSIGNMENT 12.3

Find the snapshot for The Walt Disney Company. Besides amusement parks, what other major businesses does the company own?

Detailed Description Of A Company's Operation
(For The Advanced Teenvestor)

Advanced Teenvestors who really want to understand the operations of a specific company can try the U.S. Securities and Exchange Commission (SEC). The SEC requires all U.S. companies that are traded on stock exchanges to file yearly and quarterly reports (called 10-Ks and 10-Qs, respectively) about their operations. These reports have a Business Section that can give you some insight about the business, the competition, the company's future plans, and other interesting pieces of information that can help you determine what a company does. You can get these filings from the SEC's website (www.sec.gov). Other websites take company information from the

SEC and format it to make it easier to use and understand. You will find links to these websites on www.teenvestor.com.

ASSIGNMENT 12.4

Look up the most recent 10-K report for McDonald's Corporation. Read the business analysis section.

Identifying The Competitors

In Chapter 10, we discussed the importance of identifying the industry category of a company you are considering investing in. If you recall, we stated that a comparison of companies in the same industry is a good thing because it can give you a yardstick with which to measure the company you are considering choosing. For example, if you were looking at investing in McDonald's, it makes sense to also look at how Wendy's is performing. If you have no real loyalty to McDonald's and you find that Wendy's is a better company, you may want to invest in Wendy's instead.

ASSIGNMENT 12.5

Find two competitors for each of the following companies: United Airlines, Dell Computers, and Sears.

13

EVALUATING STOCKS: LOOKING AT THE NUMBERS

This chapter is primarily to help you evaluate stable companies that have been making money for a period of five years or more. The ideas presented here can't be totally applied to high-tech companies, although the information-gathering techniques we teach you can be used for any type of company. Teenvestors interested in evaluating high-tech companies will find additional help in the next chapter. But whatever you do, don't skip this chapter!

As you go through the calculations in this chapter, keep in mind that most of the numbers you need in order to analyze a company are readily available through various investment websites. We believe, however, that you will be a better Teenvestor if you truly understand the meaning of the numbers and do some of the calculations on your own.

There is no one magical formula that will tell you whether to buy a stock or not. And despite how confident they may appear, those well-dressed experts on financial news shows can't tell you for sure whether a stock will be a looser or a winner in the future. The best anyone can do is to point you to signs that could *possibly* mean good or bad things for a company going forward. Keep all of this in mind as you go through this chapter or any other investment books.

The examples we provide in this chapter primarily center around the following five companies: PepsiCo Inc., Motorola Inc., Cisco Systems Inc., McDonald's Corporation, and Merck & Company. Please understand that by using these companies in our examples, we are not endorsing them as good investments. We just happened to choose them out of the thousands of large well-known companies available in order to illustrate the principles discussed in this chapter.

Unless otherwise stated, the financial figures you see in this chapter are the numbers available in the second quarter of 2001. We will update these figures on our website, www.teenvestor.com, as more current financial data becomes available for fiscal years 2001, 2002, 2003, and so on.

FACTS AND FIGURES ABOUT THE COMPANY

Once you have a thorough understanding of what a company does, your next step is to look at the company's financial figures. These numbers include the size of the company, its sales or revenue, its earnings, its balance sheet components, and other significant factors that can help you make a decision about whether to buy the company's stock.

Market Capitalization

Market capitalization (or *market cap*) gives you an indication of the size of a company. It is the number of shares held by the public times the current stock price. Mathematically, it is represented as follows:

Market Capitalization = (# of Shares) x (Current Stock Price)

As you can see from the above formula, the market cap of a company changes as its stock price changes. At the time of this writing, our five sample companies had the following market capitalizations:

Market Capitalization (In Billions)*

PepsiCo (PEP)	Motorola (MOT)	Cisco (CSCO)	McDonald's (MCD)	Merck (MRK)
$66.3	$32.0	$128.2	$36.4	$155.5

* Market Capitalization As of 6/22/01

Investors typically use the terms *large-cap*, *mid-cap*, *small-cap*, and *micro-cap*, to classify the size of companies. There are no clear-cut numbers for determining whether to classify a company as a large-cap, mid-cap, small-cap, or micro-cap company. The Motley Fools, a company that runs a popular investment website, suggests the following classification for the market cap of companies:

Micro-cap	below $150 million
Small-cap	$150 million to $500 million
Mid-cap	$500 million to $5 billion
Large-cap	over $5 billion

We recommend that beginning Teenvestors start with large-cap companies because the stock prices of these companies don't go up or down as much as the stock prices of smaller companies. The general rule is that the bigger a company is, the less the stock price will move up or down. The Dow consists only of large-cap stocks, which generally have stable prices over a short period of time. But of course, stable prices also mean that the stocks in The Dow don't appreciate quickly either. Over a long period of time, however, large cap shares do well. Large-cap Dow companies like Coca-Cola and General Motors *have* made some people mighty rich.

After getting your feet wet with large-cap companies, you can also try companies in the higher range of the mid-cap classification (i.e. market cap of $2.5 billion and above). We recommend that you stay away from small-caps until you're really good at doing company research (which might be three or four years from now).

Under no circumstances should you invest in micro-cap stocks (also known as *penny stocks*). Some beginning investors find penny stocks attractive because they can often be bought for less than a dollar per share. But these stocks are extremely risky; it is difficult to get reliable information about the companies that issue them or information that can tell the investor whether the stocks are good investments or not. In fact, these types of stocks are open to fraud by brokers for reasons that are beyond the topic of this book. To put it plainly, there is a good chance you will lose your money with penny stocks unless you really know what you are doing and you have a reliable source of legitimate company information.

ASSIGNMENT 13.1

List the current market caps for the following companies: Cisco Systems Inc., Chiquita Brands International, General Motors Corp., Kenneth Cole Productions, eBay Inc., and Boston Celtics LP. Put each company's stock into the market capitalization categories we discussed earlier.

Sales or Revenue

Sales (also known as *revenue*) tell you the dollar amount of goods and services a company sells. This is important because what it really tells you is the amount of money being brought into a company as a result its customers' desire for whatever the company is selling.

Growth of Sales

When evaluating the possibility of investing in a company, growth in sales is what really matters—not just the level of sales. The reason growth in sales matters is that as an investor, you want to know that the demand for a company's products or services will be increasing in the future. If the demand for a company's products or services is high, it is more likely that the company will continue to make more money in the future. And the money a company makes helps determine its stock price.

It's important for a Teenvestor to find out why big changes in sales may happen from year to year. If the change in sales is because the company sold some of its operations to another company, then a decrease in sales doesn't mean that the company is doing poorly. If the decrease in sales is because no one wants what the company is selling, then that is bad news. Because good Teenvestors invest in stocks for the long term, small decreases in sales over a one-year or two-year may be no big deal. It is important to know the underlying cause of the change but there may be no need to panic with a small decrease in sales. However, if sales have been going down steadily over the past 3 years, we recommend that you try some other company unless you have a good reason to expect a rebound.

On the other hand, sales figures could suddenly increase for a company, not because it sold more of its goods and services, but because the company purchased or merged with another company. An increase in sales due to mergers or acquisitions doesn't tell investors anything—good or bad—about the demand for a company's products or services.

Once again, as is the case in all of our analysis, you must compare the sales growth in the company you are researching with the growth in the industry. There are sites that can give you the sales growth averages in specific industries. In general, sales growth of about 10% is considered good for large-cap companies. For mid-cap and small-cap companies, sales growth of 15% to 20% or more is ideal.

ASSIGNMENT 13.2

Calculate the sales growth for Gateway Inc. (the computer company), General Motors Corp., and Johnson & Johnson for the past four years. Rank the companies in terms of the average sales growth for the past 4 years. See our site for help on calculating growth.

Cost Of Goods Sold

While sales or revenue growth is important, the cost of making those sales, referred to as *cost of sales* or *cost of goods sold (COGS)* is also very important. Keep in mind that cost of sales refers only to the cost of the materials or labor used to make the products sold or the services delivered. COGS does not include (1) *Selling, General &*

Administration Expenses or SGA—expenses not directly related to the products or services sold such as rent, lease, utilities, salary, marketing, etc., (2) *Research & Development* or R&D—investments companies make in developing new and better products or services, and (3) *Interest, Taxes, Depreciation and Amortization* or ITDA—interest on loans, taxes owed, and depreciation and amortization on buildings and equipment.

Professional investors pay close attention to the cost of sales because when it increases, it reduces a company's earnings—and earnings drive stock prices. In general, a company's sales should grow faster than its COGS.

Here is a simple example to illustrate why you have to consider the growth of COGS along with the growth in sales. Let's suppose that you run a lawn-mowing business and you rent the lawn mower each time you have a customer. You charge $50 to mow big lawns and it costs you $10 to rent the lawnmower and to fill it with gasoline. The $50 you collect for mowing a lawn is the sales or revenue and the $10 is the cost of sales. This means that each time you mow a lawn, you earn a profit of $40, which is calculated as the sales or revenue of $50 minus the cost of sales of $10 ($50-$10=$40). If your cost of renting the lawnmower goes up to $20 all of a sudden, the profit for each lawn you mow will go down to $30 ($50-$20=$30) unless you raise the price you charge. You can probably raise your price a bit, but there is a limit how much more your customers will pay for you to mow their lawns. Your customers probably won't like it if all of a sudden you raise your price by $10 and charge $60 to mow their lawns so that you can still maintain your $40 profit ($60-$20=$40). On the other hand, you can try it, but you may loose a few customers.

If you raise your price by just $5 instead of $10, so that you now charge $55, you may lose fewer customers. Your profit will be $35 ($55-$20=$35) instead of the $40 you were making originally. But if expenses keep going up, there is only so much you can do to maintain a reasonable profit in your business.

Many businesses are faced with the same dilemma of rising COGS as described in the previous example. As their COGS increase, they too have to increase their prices so that their earnings aren't significantly reduced. For many businesses, however, increasing prices to make up for higher COGS result in losing some customers. Some businesses end up compromising by raising prices somewhat (but not fully) to cover increased COGS. In the long run, the stocks of businesses whose expenses are growing faster than their revenue are not attractive investments.

ASSIGNMENT 13.3

Calculate the growth of COGS for Gateway Inc. (the computer company), General Motors Corp., and Johnson & Johnson for the past four years. Compare the COGS growth of each of these companies to the sales growth calculated in Assignment 13.2. Are there any years in which any of the companies had higher COGS than sales?

Gross Profit & Gross Margin (For The Advanced Teenvestor)

The *gross profit* (also known as *gross operating profit)* is the sales less COGS. This number divided by sales is the *gross margin* (in percentage terms). The calculations are represented mathematically as follows:

$$Gross\ Profit = Sales - COGS$$
$$Gross\ Margin = Gross\ Profit \times 100\ /\ Sales$$

The calculations above, as with most of the calculations in this book, are simple. But it is important that you understand the information you can get out of the numbers. What gross margin tells you is how profitable the business is before taking into account, the expenses not directly related to the product being sold. For example, gross profit does not consider the telephone expenses or rent in a company as part of COGS. All gross profit can tell you is whether the products being sold by a company is profitable on its own. You are likely to see high gross margins for technology and Internet companies. For example, Microsoft Corporation's gross margin is around 86%. This means that for every $1 Microsoft gets from customers, it keeps 86 cents and spends 14 cents to deliver its products or services to the customer (although the 86 cents it keeps for each dollar it takes in still has to be reduced by other indirect costs of doing business such as SG&A, R&D, and ITDA). Here are the gross margins for our five sample companies:

Gross Margin*

PEPSICo (PEP)	Motorola (MOT)	Cisco (CSCO)	McDonald's (MCD)	Merck (MRK)
61%	35%	52%	32%	43%

* Trailing Twelve-Month Gross Margin As of 6/22/01

We recommend that if Teenvestors are looking at large-cap companies, they stick to companies that have gross margins of 35% or more, unless the company is very solid in all other ways discussed in this chapter. For mid-cap firms, stick to gross margins of over 50% unless the companies have other strong features.

Net Profit & Profit Margin

The only reason most companies exist is to make money. *Net profit* (sometimes referred to as *net income*, *net earnings*, or just plain *earnings*) is how much profit a company makes after subtracting all its expenses. Mathematically, net profit is calculated as follows:

Net Profit = Sales - COGS - SG&A - R&D - ITDA

Where 1) COGS is cost of goods sold, 2) SG&A are the selling, general and administrative expenses, 3) R&D are the research and development expenses, and 4) ITDA are the interest, taxes, depreciation and amortization expenses.

When all is said and done, the price of a stock increases because investors think the company will make more money in the future. When a company's net profit grows, the investor has a better chance of receiving dividends (if the company pays dividends at all), the retained earnings grows (meaning that more money is plowed back into the company), and other investors are attracted to the company because of its success (thereby driving the stock price higher).

In the world of investing, companies whose net profit grows each year from 15%-20% (or more) are considered growth stocks. For our purposes, if a company's profit has increased by 15% or more for each of the past 5 years, and is expected to increase by about the same amount next year, you can consider it a growth stock.

Some companies that have no earnings can still make for good investments because of the anticipation of earnings. This is the only reason why some new technology and Internet companies do well from the standpoint of their stock prices. These companies typically have losses for years as they spend a lot of money to develop their technologies. But what investors are betting on is that some time in the future, they will start making money because of the technical superiority or the uniqueness of their products.

Once you have calculated net profit you can then calculate *profit margin* (also known as *net margin* or *net profit margin*), which is given in percentage terms as follows:

$$Profit\ Margin = Net\ Profit \times 100\ /\ Sales$$

While net profit numbers are important, profit margins are even more significant because they can tell you how much money a company actually keeps for each dollar it gets from its customers after paying absolutely all of its expenses. Here are the profit margins for our five sample companies:

Profit Margin*

PepsiCo (PEP)	Motorola (MOT)	Cisco (CSCO)	McDonald's (MCD)	Merck (MRK)
10.9%	.9%	-1.0%	13.2%	16.3%

* Trailing Twelve-Month Profit Margin As of 6/22/01

As with some other fundamental analysis measures, it pays to calculate net profit margin over time to see if it is steady, going down, or increasing. Ideally, you would want net profit margin to go up or stay steady. A declining profit margin is not good unless there are some unusual circumstances that caused it. For example, when a company closes a manufacturing plant, there are usually some extra expenses associated with giving the workers *severance pay*—money workers are paid when they are fired or laid off. In the year these workers are fired or laid off, the company's expenses will increase by the severance pay. But these expenses will not show up on the company's income statement in the next year so there may be no reason for alarm when the decrease in profit margin is because of such an unusual expense item. So it pays to dig deeper to find the underlying cause of decrease in profit margins.

Some industries, such as retail clothing and consumer electronics, have low profit margins. For this reason, no one can really tell you the minimum profit margin you should seek for the company whose stock you are considering buying. What's fair to say is that if you are interested in a particular industry, choose the companies in that industry that have the highest profit margins. Our website will show you how to make such comparisons within industries.

ASSIGNMENT 13.4

Assume the numbers on the table below represent the sales and expense figures on Teenvestor, Inc.'s income statement for three years. Calculate the company's net profit and profit margin for each year. Advanced Teenvestors should also calculate the gross profit and gross margin for each year. Make some comments about the change in sales, net profit, net profit margin, gross profit and gross margin from 2002 to 2004.

Teenvestor, Inc. Income Statement Items

	2002	2003	2004
Sales	$2,000,000	$2,200,000	$2,500,000
COGS	$1,000,000	$1,200,000	$1,500,000
SGA	$200,000	$200,000	$200,000
R&D	$200,000	$200,000	$200,000
Taxes	$200,000	$200,000	$200,000

ASSIGNMENT 13.5 TO 13.6

Assignment 13.5: Calculate the latest profit margin for Gateway Inc., General Motors Corp., and Johnson & Johnson. Alternatively, our site can instruct you on how to get the information from the Internet.

Assignment 13.6: Calculate the actual earnings growth for Cisco, General Motors Corp., USX, Johnson & Johnson for the past four years. Which of these companies, if any, would you consider as growth companies?

Cash And Debt

A nice chunk of cash and very little debt is always good. A company with lots of cash can survive difficult financial times brought on by bad business conditions. In addition, the company can use the cash to expand or improve its operations when the opportunity arises. A low debt amount means that the company's money is not wasted on interest payments.

Debt-Equity Ratios

There are simple calculations you can perform to find out about a company's debt and how much cash it can get its hand on when it runs into an emergency. One such calculation is called the *debt-equity ratio* (sometimes shown in percentage format and sometimes shown in decimal format). The debt-equity ratio is the ratio of long-term debt to equity (or common stock or shareholder's equity). Recall that in Chapter 3 we defined long-term debt as a loan that is due to be paid back in over one year. This figure can be found in the long-term liability section of a company's balance sheet. The equity, which represents the investments in the company by its owners, can usually be found near the end of a company's balance sheet. The mathematical representation of the debt-equity ratio when shown in decimal format is:

Debt-Equity Ratio = Long-Term Debt / Equity

When represented in percentage format, the debt-equity ratio is calculated as follows:

Debt-Equity Ratio = Long-Term Debt x 100 / Equity

The higher the debt-equity ratio, the more money the company has borrowed. And of course, the higher the borrowed amount, the higher the interest payment, which is really just another expense, as we explained earlier.

If you recall our SportsTee example in Chapter 3, the partners of the company contributed a total of $2,500 (the equity) and borrowed $1,000 ($400 or which was long-term debt and $600 of which was short-term debt). For SportsTee, the debt-equity ratio was $400/$2500 = .16 or 16%.

Some industries are known for borrowing more money than other industries. The construction and telecommunications industries are two great examples of industries that traditionally carry lots of debt.

We recommend that you stay clear of companies with debt-equity ratios of .50 or more over several years. If you find that the company in which you want to invest belongs to an industry that normally has a high debt-equity ratio, make sure that company has one of the lowest debt-equity ratios in that industry group.

Here are the debt-equity ratios for our five sample companies:

Debt-Equity Ratio*				
PepsiCo (PEP)	Motorola (MOT)	Cisco (CSCO)	McDonald's (MCD)	Merck (MRK)
.33	.40	0.00	.88	.24

* Debt-Equity Ratio for Most Recent Quarter As of 6/22/01

Notice that Cisco, like many technology companies, has a very low (or zero) debt-equity ratio.

In addition to looking at the current level of the debt-equity ratio, it is also good to look at how this ratio changes over time. Compare the debt-equity ratio for the company over a 5-year period. In general, a falling debt-equity ratio means that the company is paying off some of the loans it has taken out. This is usually good news for people who want to invest in the company.

Current Ratio

Another measurement that can tell you whether a company will be able to pay what it owes is the *current ratio*, which uses current assets and current liabilities in its calculation. In Chapter 4 we discussed current assets and current liabilities. Just to refresh your memory, a current asset is an asset that is due the company within one year. For example, the current asset on a company's balance sheet could be its certificates of deposits, or CDs as they are called—a short-term loan to a bank. Current liabilities are liabilities due in less than one year. Examples could be a loan the company takes out which is due in 3 months. The current ratio, which is usually shown in decimal format, is current assets divided by current liabilities. The calculation is as follows:

Current Ratio = Current Assets / Current Liabilities

In general, the higher the current ratio, the better off the company because it indicates that the company can afford to pay its immediate bills. For example, a current ratio of 2 is better than a current ratio of 1. Once again, look at the current ratio of other companies in the same industry as the company you are investigating. If the current ratio is around the same level as the other companies, you are probably in good shape.

In addition, look at the growth or decrease in the current ratio. A steady decrease in the current ratio over the past 3 to 5 years could spell trouble. Here are the current ratios for our five sample companies:

Current Ratio*

PepsiCo (PEP)	Motorola (MOT)	Cisco (CSCO)	McDonald's (MCD)	Merck (MRK)
1.2	1.4	1.6	.7	1.2

* Current Ratio for Most Recent Quarter As of 6/22/01

Think for a minute about what these numbers mean. Cisco's current ratio of 1.6 for example, means that it has 1.6 times more short-term assets to pay off any debt that will come due in the next one to twelve months.

Return on Equity

Return on equity (ROE) is the best way to learn how much money a company is making for its investors. It is calculated by dividing the company's net profit by its equity. It is represented mathematically (in percentage terms) as follows:

$$ROE = Net\ Profit \times 100\ /\ Equity$$

ROE can reveal how much money the company is making compared with how much it has invested to make that money. Just to use a simple example, if you invest $100 in a rare baseball card and sell it for $120, your net profit will be $20 ($120 - $100 = $20), and your ROE would be $20/$100 or 20%. The $100 in the denominator is your equity in the card business. The 20% ROE represents your percentage return on that $100 investment. The ROE is the same as the "return on investment" concept we discussed in Chapter 10 since "investment" is really just another term for equity. Here are the ROEs for our five sample companies:

ROE*

PepsiCo (PEP)	Motorola (MOT)	Cisco (CSCO)	McDonald's (MCD)	Merck (MRK)
32.3%	1.7%	-.9%	21.0%	51.3%

* Trailing Twelve-Month ROE As of 6/22/01

When looking at a company, it is important to look at the trend in ROE to make sure that it is not steadily declining. Experienced investors sometimes look at the ROE of other companies in the same industry to make sure that the ROE of the company they are looking at is in line with its competitors'.

In Chapter 10 we discussed one of the basic investment strategies many investors use in choosing stock: value investing. Value investors tend to look for bargains in the stock market. That is, they look for companies that are temporarily doing poorly or not living up to their promise but (hopefully) will soon become more profitable. One of the ways they determine if a stock's poor performance is temporary is to take a careful look at its historical ROEs. The logic goes something like this: if the average ROE in the past five years has been 20% and the ROE for the last year was 10%, there is a good chance that the ROE may get back to its old 20% level sometime in the future. For a long-term investor this logic may work, but it may not work for a short-term investor (which we hope you are not).

Earnings per Share

Earnings per share, or EPS, is the amount of money the company actually earns for each share of stock held by investors. It is calculated, in dollars per share, as follows:

EPS = Net Profit / (#Of Common Shares Outstanding)

Ideally, EPS should increase each year. Here are the EPS figures for our five sample companies available at the time of this writing:

EPS*

PepsiCo (PEP)	Motorola (MOT)	Cisco (CSCO)	McDonald's (MCD)	Merck (MRK)
2.97	.14	-.04	1.43	2.55

* Trailing Twelve-Month EPS As of 6/22/01

As discussed earlier, companies report their earnings for each quarter—in other words, every three months. Just before companies announce their quarterly earnings to the world, investment analysts make predictions about the amount of money these companies will make for each share of stock outstanding for the current quarter and for the year (or years) to come. This information can give you a good idea about what the best minds on Wall Street think of certain companies.

Wall Street analysts publish their best EPS estimates for big, publicly traded companies. When these companies finally report their earnings, most investors usually compare the Wall Street analysts' projections with the companies' actual EPS figures for the quarter. If actual EPS figures are more than the Wall Street analysts' projections, even by 10 cents a share, the stock price of the companies usually go up. Stock prices can also go down when actual EPS figures are less than the predicted amounts.

Teenvestors are surprised when they find out that even small differences between predicted EPS numbers and actual EPS numbers can influence the stock prices of companies. To make sense of it, they have to consider what the differences say about the profitability of these companies. For example, PepsiCo has about 1.46 billion shares in the hands of investors. If the company's EPS is 10 cents less than predicted by analysts, it means that its earnings were about 146 million dollars (10 cents x 1.46 billion shares = $146 million) less than was expected—a big number even for a company like PepsiCo. As you can see, this EPS difference makes a clear statement that the company is not making as much money as was predicted. And because expectations can affect stock prices (as we discussed in Chapter 9), any difference between expectations and reality is likely to affect the price of any stock.

We recommend that Teenvestors ignore analysts' EPS projections for the current quarter and focus on long-term projections and the reasons why those projections were made. What should matter to you is what the analysts feel the stock will do in the next year or two.

See if their logic makes sense to you; invest for the future, not the present.

ASSIGNMENT 13.7

Find the debt-equity ratio, current ratio, ROE, and EPS for Gateway Inc., General Motors Corp., and Johnson & Johnson for the past 5 years. See our website for help.

Price-Earnings Ratio

The *price-earnings ratio*, or PE (also known as PE ratio), is one of those topics that we have to discuss, not because it is so important to Teenvestors, but because a lot of other investors focus on it. The PE is one way investors determine how much a stock costs compared with how much profit the company makes. The PE is today's price of the stock divided by the EPS of the company over the past year. Mathematically, it is calculated as follows:

$$PE = \text{Today's Price Per Share} / EPS$$

Like most of the data in this chapter, PE can be found in a number of good financial websites. The way to interpret PE is that it tells you how many years it will take for you to get back your investment if you buy one share of a company's stock (and all of the company's net profit each year gets distributed as dividends). By way of example, suppose you buy a share of Teenvestor Inc. at $30 and the yearly EPS (earnings per share) is $2. This means that the first year after buying the stock, you would earn $2. You'd earn another $2 for the second year; and another $2 for the third year. If we keep going, you will see that it would take 15 years to earn back a total of $30—your initial investment. You could have figured out how long it would take to earn back the $30 investment by dividing the stock price by the earnings per share ($30/$2 = 15).

Investors refer to stock as either cheap or expensive based on PE levels. For a given stock, a PE of, say, 20 is more expensive than a PE of 15. Some value investors believe that over a long period of time, the PE ratios of companies stay stable, so they watch PEs to see when it is cheap for them to buy the stock. For example, if the PE ratio of Teenvestor Inc. has been 50 for the past 10 years, and is suddenly 30, these value investors will buy more of Teenvestor Incorporated's stock in hopes that the PE ratio will move back up to 50, meaning that the stock price may go back up. But one major flaw in focusing solely on PE ratios is that the PE ratio of a stock can increase even if that stock's price does not change very much. If EPS goes down, the PE ratio can go up. What this means is that if you buy Teenvestor Inc.'s stock when it has a PE ratio of 30, and it later goes to a PE ratio of 50, it would not necessarily mean that the company's stock price went up. It could mean that earnings per share went down, without an equivalent change in the value of the stock. Still, a PE ratio can serve as a general guide as to whether a stock is more expensive or cheaper relative to its earnings.

Growth stocks (or companies whose earnings grow by 20% or more per year over several years) usually have high PE ratios. PE ratios are typically high for technology and Internet companies, if they make money at all. For example, at the height of the Internet boom in 2000, the PE ratio for eBay, the online auction house, was over 2300.

This high level of PE was not really meaningful to investors since the only reason it was so big was because eBay was making very little money at that time. In other words, eBay's tiny earnings at that time, which is used in the denominator of the PE formula (Price Per Share / Earnings Per Share) made the ratio very big. To drive the point home, what will be the PE ratio of a company that has no earnings? Mathematically, when you divide any stock price by 0 (which represents no earnings), you will get an infinite number. Of course, an infinite PE ratio is meaningless. For new industries (such as the industries created from the Internet), you can't use the PE ratio as a measure of whether companies are cheap or expensive until these companies have had positive earnings over a 3 to 5-year period. And even then, using PE ratios as the only way to spot bargains in technology stocks is flawed. (See Chapter 14 for information on evaluating high-tech companies). Here are the PE ratios for our five sample companies available at the time of this writing:

PE Ratio*

PepsiCo (PEP)	Motorola (MOT)	Cisco (CSCO)	McDonald's (MCD)	Merck (MRK)
30	64	192	22	28

* Trailing Twelve-Month PE Ratio As of 6/22/01

ASSIGNMENT 13.8

Find the PE ratios of Dell Computer Corporation, General Motors Corporation, and McDonald's Corporation for the past 5 years.

Our website, www.teenvestor.com, contains more information on the various calculations that will help you spot quality stocks.

14

EVALUATING HIGH-TECH AND INTERNET STOCKS

Technology companies have a financial and emotional appeal that some investors can't resist. On the financial level, technology investors dream of discovering the next Microsoft or America Online. On the emotional side, the thought of whiz-bang electronic gadgets or health-improving bio-technological techniques and products to help us live fuller lives is very attractive. But here are the problems:

1. *What is considered high-tech today could easily become ho-hum tomorrow.* There was a time, for example, when simply putting up a website was considered a big deal. Now, 12-year-old children are putting up their own sites, complete with streaming video and audio clips.

2. *It is sometimes difficult to understand exactly what some high-tech companies do.* Can anyone truly say she understands the issues surrounding the sequencing of the human DNA?

Unless you are investing in the biggest technology companies in America, high-technology stocks move up and down more quickly than those of other industries. For proof, you need to look no further than the fluctuations in the NASDAQ Composite Index. The NASDAQ Index, which most often reflects the change in the value of technology stocks and Internet stocks, had record gains and record losses in 2000. In other words, its value swung wildly. The Dow went up and down too, but not by as much on a daily basis. All this is to say that investing in technology is generally riskier than investing in traditional companies such as the McDonald's Corporation or General Motors Corporation.

We should tell you that we feel Teenvestors should stay away from all but the biggest technology companies in America. Even for the big, more stable high-technology companies, Teenvestors should put no more than 1/5th of their money in these stocks.

This chapter will lay out some general guidelines about how to evaluate technology companies.

THE DIFFERENCE BETWEEN HIGH-TECH AND INTERNET COMPANIES

There *is* a difference between high-technology and Internet stocks although many investors tend to lump them together. High-technology stocks can be roughly described as the stocks of companies that (1) use advanced technology to make their products or offer their services, or (2) sell technically advanced products or services. A company such as Palm (which makes the Palm Pilot, the electronic address book, calendar, and Internet device) can be considered a technology company.

An Internet-based company may just be using the Internet to deliver goods and services that have been traditionally sold in retail stores or in other physical locations. One could argue that Amazon.com is not a technology company but, rather, that it is primarily a bookstore in cyberspace (although it is branching out into many different businesses).

One thing high-technology and Internet companies do have in common is that, for most investors, some of the newly formed companies that fall into these categories are difficult (or nearly impossible) to evaluate. For the purposes of this chapter, we lump high-technology and Internet companies together.

THE TEMPTATION TO DIVE INTO HIGH-TECH AND INTERNET STOCKS

At some point in your life as a Teenvestor, you will be tempted to buy technology and Internet stocks in hopes of making fast money. Sooner or later, the phrase Initial Public Offerings (IPOs) will make you drool. We recommend that Teenvestors stay away from Internet stocks until the companies issuing these stocks begin to show net earnings instead of just revenue. At the time of this writing, only a precious handful of Internet-based companies are making any profit. In fact, one of the strongest Internet companies, America Online, which was started in 1985, began making profits in 1996.

The same goes for pure-technology companies. We advise Teenvestors to stick to the strongest technology companies such as Cisco Systems, Oracle, and others that have established earnings track records.

In the case of companies issuing IPOs, we recommend that Teenvestors wait at least 18 months after their IPOs before even considering an investment. To see why caution is necessary, take a look at what happened with the IPO of Palm (a subsidiary of 3Com). Palm went public in 2000, offering 23 million shares of its stock to the public at a price of $38. On the day of the company's IPO, the price of its stock went up to $165 and then settled to $95 by the time the stock market closed. Here is a dose of the truth about this IPO: the people who bought at a price of $38 were probably not small investors; they were most likely brokerage firms and other institutions that buy up IPOs first before ordinary investors even get a whiff. You can be assured that many small investors, like you, probably bought at $165 and held on for dear life, hoping that the price went up further; but of course, on that day, the price ended up at $95.

Palm is just one example of how the IPO game for technology stocks (indeed, for any stock) is stacked against you. It is just one of countless examples of technology companies that are hyped just enough to get you interested, but in the end prices drop to rock bottom after you have made your investment.

If you learn nothing else in this chapter, you should know that whenever new technologies are introduced, a lot of competitors dive in to offer the same items. According to *The New York Times*, over 3,000 car companies were formed between 1900 and 1925. Today, there are only 3 U.S. car companies. What this should tell you is that a lot of companies that have joined the technological and Internet revolution, just won't make it.

Hundreds of Internet companies have already crashed but one of the most dramatic crashes happened in 2001 when Webvan, an online grocery delivery company, announced that it would cease operations. After Webvan was formed in 1999, its share price went as high as $34 per share. This amounted to a market capitalization of $10 billion. By July 2001 the company had spent over $830 million that it raised from investors and its shares were trading for as low as six cents per share. That's when the company filed for bankruptcy.

You should wait a little while before you decide which of these Internet and technology companies have the best chance of thriving in the next 20, 40, 60 years and beyond. These are the companies that deserve your precious money.

Having said all this, we know that like many of the Teenvestors we have met, you will probably still be tempted to buy unproven technology and Internet stocks anyway. But before you go charging off into high-tech land, the rest of this chapter will give you an idea of the things you should look for and avoid.

HOW TO INVEST IN HIGH-TECH AND INTERNET STOCKS

The traditional ways of determining whether a stock is worth buying don't always work with high-technology and Internet stocks. One reason is that many of these companies make heavy investments in research and technology when they first start operating and it can take several years before they start receiving the benefits of their research, in terms of profit. In addition, the balance sheets of these companies will reveal very few fixed assets. This is because their assets are really knowledge assets (or intellectual assets, as we discussed in Chapter 5) that can't really be shown on a balance sheet as can assets like farming tractors or 18-wheel trucks. An example of a knowledge asset is a hot-shot computer programmer who is responsible for writing a company's best-selling software. Her true value can't be represented on a balance sheet.

Many high-tech companies have losses for years before they start making any money. Take Amazon.com for example. The company has been losing money since it was founded in 1995. In 2001, it announced that it would turn a profit in 2002. Another example we mentioned earlier, AOL, made no profits until 1996 even though it has been in operation since 1985. But the company was spending a lot of money on technology to improve its services to its customers. The strategy paid off because the high value of its stock price allowed it to acquire Time Warner in one of the biggest mergers ever.

When a company has no profits or has losses year after year, you can't really calculate PE ratios, EPS, or some of the other important financial measures used to determine investment worthiness. So how can a Teenvestor determine if it is worth investing in high-tech companies making little or no money? There are several things you should consider when making this determination and they are described below.

Find Out Exactly What The Company Does

In the high-tech and Internet world, what a company does and how it intends to thrive is known as its *business model*. Financial experts such as Peter Lynch and Warren Buffett—giants in the investment community—have preached the philosophy of understanding the business models of companies before making investments. The problem is that when you start talking about high-tech and Internet companies, investors sometimes find it hard to put their minds around what the company actually does. Sure, for a company like Ebay, which is an auction website where people put up items for sale, the business model is easy to understand. But what about a company like Nokia? The company has plans to have its cell phones also serve as a device for accessing the Internet and for communicating with others in innovative ways. The typical investor probably doesn't know much about the technology and the competitors in that industry. The only solution to this problem is that, as a high-tech investor, you have to do a lot more research about the companies you are looking to invest in.

When the Internet first became commercialized, there were those who started coining phrases about the types of businesses that will be successful over the world-wide-web. One of the first popular phrases was *business-to-consumer* to indicate an Internet business that sells items to consumers. Once upon a time, investment analysts felt that business-to-consumer Internet businesses would be successful simply because of the sheer number of consumers that would be drawn to websites. The excitement over business-to-consumer Internet companies quickly faded and was replaced by enthusiasm for *business-to-business* Internet companies—companies that specialize in selling to other businesses.

We can go on and on about the various fads and trends that have been so hyped by the media. However, the bottom line is that since the Internet is so new, no one can really say if there is only one good business model. Therefore it makes sense to look at each business on its own to decide whether, in the long run, it can show enough profits to justify its stock price. The following are suggestions on how to begin evaluating the business models of high-tech companies.

Look At The SEC 10-K or 10-Q

The first thing you must do is to get a copy of a Securities and Exchange Commission (SEC) 10-K report and read the Business Section to try to make sense of the business. In Chapter 12, we discussed how to get this document but we said it was for the advanced Teenvestor. Well, if you are investing in high-tech and Internet companies that have no significant net earnings or track records, you are creeping into the territory of advanced Teenvestors. If you are not up to reading the 10-K or other documents filed by these companies, then you should stay out of the high-tech waters entirely.

Search The Archives Of Technology And Internet Publications

Use the Internet's search engine to look for information on these companies. Try searching the archives of the business sections of some reputable (and free) online newspapers such as *The New York Times* and *The Los Angeles Times*. Go to the sites of popular technology magazines such as *Red Herring, Industry Standard*, and *Business 2.0* and search their archives for your companies of choice. Even if you can't find a mention of the companies you are looking for in the archives of these publications, look up the general topic. In the case of Nokia, for example, you could look up cell phones, or one of Nokia's competitors, Ericsson.

Get Information From Your Parents' Full-Service Broker

Many full-service brokers like Merrill Lynch, for example, have access to research papers on specific companies and industries. If your parents have a full-service broker, have them ask their broker if he or she can get a report for them on the high-tech or Internet company in which you are interested.

Pay For Research Information

In this book so far, we have steered Teenvestors away from sites that charge for information. However, when it comes to high-tech and Internet companies, we will slightly violate this principle by recommending that Teenvestors buy research information before they make any serious investment in such companies. There are companies like Multex Investor, TheStreet.com, and Hoover's, through which you can buy reports on specific industries and companies.

On our website, www.teenvestor.com, you will find links to other sites where you can buy good company research or just get reliable information about high-tech companies. If you can't afford to spend the small amount of money to pay for research reports, then you'd better have another way of learning about the high-tech and Internet companies in which you want to invest.

Consider High-Tech And Internet Mutual Funds

A Teenvestor who has no clue as to how to begin looking at high-tech stocks should consider technology mutual funds. Of course, you know the major problem with investing in any mutual fund: the minimum investment balance can be several thousand dollars. Occasionally, however, you can find funds with minimum investments of around $250 or so. Index funds in the technology and Internet sectors may be the best bet for advanced Teenvestors.

Evaluate Whether The Company Has A Good Idea

Quite often, even a high-tech or Internet company that is making no money will find its stock prices going higher and higher. Sometimes, the reason these stock prices run up is that the investors think that the company has a good idea and that it is the first to offer its products to the public. Being first in a business, particularly an Internet business is called *first mover advantage*. Priceline.com, for example, which offers a site where you can name your own price on flight tickets (and groceries, and other items), has a great business idea and has "first mover advantage" in its business. Amazon.com, which sells books online, was one of the early online bookstores. AOL, which offers customers an easy way to get on the Internet, also has a great business model. All these companies had good ideas; what's more, they were among the first companies to carry out their ideas on such a big scale. But beware of companies that have a "me-too" business model—a business model that just copies what other companies in the same business are doing. An example is the Internet-based printing industry, which at the time of this writing, has seen over 35 newly formed companies with nearly identical business models.

Look For Unique Products That Others Can't Copy

Some technology and Internet companies have *patents* on their products. A patent gives inventors the sole right to make a particular product. It is a right given by the government to companies that have proven that their products or services are unique. In the past few years, companies on the Internet have even registered patents on the ease of use of their websites. In the non-Internet world, one patent you may be familiar with is the patent for the Coca-Cola soft drink formula.

Consider Qualcomm, a company that had an incredible 2,619% increase in its stock price in 1999. One of the reasons for the increase in Qualcomm's stock price was that it received one of the patents for technology that allowed consumers to access the Internet through its cell phones. The company's stock price has since experienced a steep decline, for reasons we can't explore here, but the mere announcement of the cellular phone technology initially gave it a big boost. In your search for valuable high-tech companies in which to invest, look for companies that have significant patents in their industry categories.

Avoid Businesses That Depend Solely On Selling Advertising

At the beginning of the Internet revolution, a lot of companies popped up with websites offering free information and discounted products to consumers. However, many of these companies knew that they could not really make enough money from sales of items on their sites. Instead, they hoped to make money by selling advertisement space on their websites. Specifically, they counted on banner advertisement to make money because they felt they could attract enough "eyeballs"—people who will log on to their sites—to make it worth an advertiser's money.

The reality of the Internet world, however, is that with the exception of AOL (which, at the time of this writing, has over 22 million subscribers) and a few other sites, the "eyeballs" are hard to turn into dollars. Many online companies find it hard to make ends meet by just offering banner ads for advertisers. Just think of how often you click on an advertisement at the sites you visit. We almost never do!

Stay Away From Internet-Based Businesses That Want To Offer Everything To Everyone

One of the reasons the Internet is so attractive is that you can get specific information at the click of a button. But a lot of Internet companies have been launched in the past 5 years as "generic portals"—sites that offer everything but the kitchen sink.

In short, if you want to invest in an online company offering items to consumers, we recommend you look for ones that cater to specific groups like photography buffs, art lovers, and other product or geographical groups.

Look For Traditional Companies With New Internet Initiatives

When some investors think about investing in companies that have put their businesses on the Internet, they overlook traditional companies that have recently established an online presence. In the past few years, it has become increasingly clear that traditional companies that already have warehouses and stores have some advantages over purely online companies. For one thing, traditional companies already understand distribution and customer service. They have the mechanisms to handle returned goods when customers aren't happy and they keep a lot of items on hand to cut down on time spent acquiring the goods that customers want.

During the Christmas of 1999, the first Christmas in which online shopping was considered a real option for most consumers, a lot of customers were upset at how some online companies filled their orders in terms of speed and customer service. One of the things that got customers really mad was that they couldn't easily return items they'd purchased. Refunds and other customer services are where traditional companies have big advantages over businesses that sell items strictly online because customers can return items to a real store without hassles. When traditional companies start developing their online stores that work hand-in-hand with their real stores, they will fill-in the customer service gaps left by companies who only operate online.

Any Teenvestor who is interested in investing in Internet businesses should consider traditional companies like General Motors, Wal-Mart, Citigroup, Time Warner (which has merged with AOL) and other traditional companies that have awakened to the fact that they have the warehouses, the distribution channels, and customer service know-how to build online businesses.

Our website, www.teenvestor.com, contains more information on high-tech companies, including website links through which you can get information on technology and Internet businesses.

15

UNDERSTANDING
MUTUAL FUNDS

Let's suppose that you have $500 to invest in the stock market. However, you are concerned that you might lose too much of your money if you put it all in the stock of one company. So, you decide that you would like to spread your investment into several companies. In other words, you want to diversify your investment as we described in Chapter 10. Of course, to diversify your investments, you have to put your money in the shares of companies in different industries so that if the shares of one company you invest in go down, other companies whose shares you are holding may be able to make up for this decrease if they go up in value.

Because $500 is not really enough money with which to diversify your investment, you find three other friends who have $500 each and pool your combined $2,000 ($500 from you and a total of $1,500 from your other three friends). With the $2,000, you purchase about $500 worth of stock in each of 4 companies in different industries, such as the pharmaceutical, banking, computer and automobile industries. Each of the four people who contributed to the pool of $2,000 owns 1/4th or 25% of the investments you have made with the money. This means that each person owns 25% of the dividends, and 25% of the capital appreciation (or the increase in the value of the stock). When the investments are *liquidated*—that is, when the shares are sold—each person who contributed gets 25% of the amount for which you sell the shares.

The collective investment you have made with the $2,000 pool of cash is really a *mutual fund*. This chapter explains the basics of mutual fund investing—how a mutual fund works, what factors to consider before investing, and how to avoid common pitfalls.

GENERAL INFORMATION ABOUT MUTUAL FUNDS

A mutual fund is a company that brings together money from many people and invests it in stocks, bonds, or other financial assets (or *securities*, as they are collectively known). The combined holdings of stocks, bonds, or other assets the fund owns are known as its *portfolio*. Each investor owns shares, which represent a portion of these holdings. In the example of your investment of $2,000 in the stocks of companies in four industries, each investor owned 1/4th of the investment.

There are many different types of funds. There are funds that invest in technology, foreign, small-cap or any other variety of stocks you can think of. What all funds have in common is that they all need *portfolio managers*. These managers are responsible for buying stocks and other securities for mutual funds. They are also responsible for selling and substituting securities in the fund as well. Professional management of mutual funds is the main reason a lot of investors buy mutual funds in the first place. These investors feel that they themselves just don't have the time or the skill to determine which stocks to buy on their own.

A fund can own as few as 20 different stocks or as many as 500 different stocks. There is no limit to the market value of the stocks in mutual funds. At the time of this writing, the biggest mutual fund had assets worth nearly $100 billion. This number changes depending on what is happening in the economy. More people put money in mutual funds during a bull market and move their investments to safer investments when the economy is doing poorly.

Mutual funds usually publish the amount of money they make for investors each year in order to attract more investors. The amount they make for the investors is called the fund's *annualized total return*. Funds often publish their 1-year, 3-year, 5-year, and 10-year annualized total return to boast about how much they have increased investors' money. They also publish their calendar-year total returns. For example, one of the biggest mutual funds in the world, the Vanguard 500 Index, with nearly $81 billion in assets, had the following returns for 1996 to 2000: 22.9%, 33.2%, 28.6%, 21.1%, and -9.1%.

Advertisements, rankings, and ratings tell you how well a fund has performed in the past. The more you study mutual funds, however, the more you will realize that a fund's past performance is not as important as you might think. Studies show that future returns can be quite different from historical returns. This year's "number one" fund can easily become next year's below-average fund.

PROBLEMS WITH MUTUAL FUNDS

We want to tell you from the outset that mutual funds are not as Teenvestor-friendly as individual stocks. For one thing, most mutual funds require initial investments that range from $1,000 to $3,000. On occasion, you can find some investment plans that require $50 to $100 monthly until you hit the minimum investment amount. But how many Teenvestors really have that kind of cash on hand every month?

Another reason why we don't think mutual funds are Teenvestor-friendly is that figuring out how much tax you owe on the money you make with your mutual fund investments can be complicated. If you own many varieties of mutual funds and you buy and sell shares frequently, you and your parents will probably have to consult an accountant.

Despite our opinion about the problems of Teenvestors investing in mutual funds, we feel that we should still cover how to go about choosing funds just in case you have the cash to do it and you can get help to fill out your tax forms (if you buy and sell shares frequently). If you *do* choose to invest in mutual funds, you should stick to those funds that invest in stocks since, as we discussed earlier, stocks generally can make more money for you over a long period of time.

THE ADVANTAGES OF MUTUAL FUNDS

Mutual funds can be a good way for Teenvestors to invest in stocks and bonds (if they can overcome the obstacles mentioned above) for the following reasons:

1. mutual funds are managed by professional money managers;

2. by owning shares in a mutual fund instead of buying individual stocks or bonds directly, you spread out your investment risk; and

3. because a mutual fund buys and sells large amounts of stocks and bonds (and other financial assets) at a time, its costs are often lower than what you would pay on your own.

NET ASSET VALUE

When we speak of the value of a share of stock, we say that it is worth a specific dollar amount. The value of a share in a mutual fund is referred to as its Net Asset Value per share or NAV. When you buy mutual fund shares, you pay the current NAV per share, plus any sales charge (also called a *sales load*). When you sell your shares, the fund will pay you the total NAV value at the time of the sale, less any other sales load. A fund's NAV goes up or down daily as the value of the individual stocks in the fund changes.

As an example, suppose you invest $1,000 in a mutual fund with an NAV of $10. You will therefore own 100 shares of the fund. If, after you make your investment, the NAV of the mutual fund drops to $9 (because the value of the fund's portfolio has dropped), you will still own 100 shares, but your investment will be worth $900. If after you make your investment, the NAV goes up to $11, your investment will be worth $1,100. This example assumed no sales charge.

KINDS OF MUTUAL FUNDS

You take risks when you invest in any mutual fund. You may lose some or all of the money you invest (your principal) because the value of the stocks (or securities) held by a fund goes up and down.

Each kind of mutual fund has different risks. Generally, the higher the potential return (the money you can make), the higher the risk of loss.

Before you invest, decide whether the goals and risks of any fund you are considering are a good fit for you. To make this decision, you may need the help of a financial adviser. There are also investment books and services to guide you.

The three main categories of mutual funds are money market funds, bond funds, and stock funds. There are a variety of types within each category.

Money Market Funds

Money market funds have relatively low risks, compared with other mutual funds. They are limited by law to certain high-quality, short-term investments. Money market funds try to keep their value (NAV) at a stable $1.00 per share, but NAV may fall below $1.00 if their investments perform poorly. Investor losses on money market funds have been rare, but they are possible.

Bond Funds

Bond funds (also called *fixed income funds*) have higher risks than money market funds, but seek to pay higher returns. Unlike money market funds, bond funds are not restricted to high-quality or short-term investments. Because there are many different types of bonds, bond funds can vary dramatically in their risks.

Most bond funds have credit risk, which is the risk that companies or other issuers whose bonds are owned by the fund may fail to pay their debts (including the debt owed to holders of their bonds). Some funds have little credit risk, such as those that invest in government bonds. But be careful: nearly all bond funds have interest-rate risk, which means that the value of the bonds they hold will go down when interest rates go up. Because of this, you can lose money in any bond fund, including those that invest only in government bonds.

Long-term bond funds invest in bonds with longer *maturities* (length of time until the final payout). The values (NAVs) of long-term bond funds can go up or down more rapidly than those of short-term bond funds.

Stock Funds

Stock funds (also called *equity funds*) generally involve more risk than money market or bond funds, but they also can offer the highest returns (or the highest profit). A stock fund's value (NAV) can rise and fall quickly over the short term, but historically stocks have performed better over the long term than other types of investments.

Not all stock funds are the same. For example, *growth* funds focus on stocks that may not pay a regular dividend but have the potential to increase in value. Others specialize in a particular industry segment such as technology stocks.

Stock funds are more appropriate for Teenvestors than bond funds.

THE THREE WAYS YOU CAN EARN MONEY WITH FUNDS

You can earn money from your mutual fund investment in three ways. First, a fund may receive income in the form of dividends and interest on the securities it owns. A fund will pay its shareholders nearly all of the income it has earned in the form of dividends.

Second, the price of the securities a fund owns may increase—this is known as capital appreciation, as explained in Chapter 10. When a fund sells a security that has increased in price, the fund has a capital gain. At the end of the year, most funds distribute these capital gains to investors.

Third, if a fund does not sell but, instead, holds on to securities that have increased in price, the value of its shares (NAV) increases. The higher NAV reflects the higher value of your investment. If you sell your shares, you make a profit (and this is also a capital gain).

Usually funds will give you a choice: the fund can send you the *distributions* (capital gains and dividends), or you can have them *re-invested* in the fund to buy more shares, often without paying an additional sales load.

GETTING INFORMATION ON MUTUAL FUNDS

There are sources of information that you should consult before you invest in mutual funds. The most important of these is the fund's *prospectus*. The prospectus is the fund's selling document and contains information about costs, risks, past performance, and the fund's investment goals.

Request a prospectus from a fund, or from a financial professional if you are using one. Read the prospectus before you invest. Check the fund's annualized total returns (sometimes called just "total returns" in the prospectus). You will find it in the Financial Highlights, near the front of the prospectus.

Observe how total return has varied over the years. The Financial Highlights in the prospectus show yearly total return for the most recent 10 year period. An impressive 10-year total return may be based on one spectacular year followed by many average years. Looking at year-to-year changes in total return is a good way to see how stable the fund's returns have been.

THINGS TO CONSIDER WHEN CHOOSING AND INVESTING IN A FUND

You can buy some mutual funds by contacting them directly. Others are sold mainly through brokers, banks, financial planners, or insurance agents. All mutual funds will *redeem* (or buy back) your shares on any business day and must send you the payment within seven days. Just as with stocks, however, you can't buy mutual funds unless you are at least 18 years old. Your parents have to establish a special account called a *custodial account* for you in order for you to buy any mutual funds. See Chapter 19 for more information on custodial accounts.

Even though we don't think mutual funds are very Teenvestor-friendly, the following sections will help to point you to the right type of funds in which to invest and help you to stay away from the funds that are too risky.

Stick With A Simple Strategy

Teenvestors should not invest in funds they don't really understand. The following suggestions should help you keep things simple.

Index Funds

A lot of mutual funds spend a lot of time and money trying to choose the right stocks for their portfolios. Fund managers choose stocks that they think will go up in price and dump stocks that they think will go down in price. These types of funds are called *actively managed* funds because someone actually has to watch the fund carefully to determine whether to buy or sell the fund's assets. These actively managed funds charge investors a lot of money for their efforts in trying to increase the value of the funds. The dirty little secret though in mutual funds is that there are funds that need no managers, and yet still do very well. These types of funds are called *index funds*. The most common index funds are made up of stocks in the S&P 500. (Recall that that the stocks in the S&P 500 are 500 of the biggest companies in the country). Another common index fund is a fund that mirrors the Wilshire 5000—an index which reflects the U.S. stock market.

In the past few years, index funds made up of the S&P 500 stocks did better than 95% of all stock funds. When you stop to think about it, this is really a shocking fact. What this says is that a mutual fund that does nothing but hold S&P 500 stocks does better on the average than most funds that are actively managed by hot-shot Wall

Street geniuses. There is no guarantee that index funds that are not actively managed will continue to perform better than nearly all actively managed funds. Nevertheless, index funds make for an easy choice for Teenvestors who don't want to knock themselves out choosing funds out of the thousands available.

Teenvestors should try index funds—at least when they start off investing in mutual funds. Three big index funds to consider are the following: the Vanguard 500 Index, the Vanguard Total Stock Market Index, and the T. Rowe Price Equity Index 500. You can find many more index funds through our website.

Teenvestor-Friendly Funds

Even though most funds are very expensive to invest in, there are a few funds that are suitable for Teenvestors. One prominent Teenvestor-friendly fund is the Stein Roe Young Investor fund. The fund managers say the fund invests in companies that young people know such as America Online, Walt Disney, and General Electric. A more careful look at the fund, however, shows that it has plenty of stocks that young people won't recognize. In our mind, the real value of the fund is that with a custodial account, you can invest sums in the amount of $50 per month instead of the $1,000 to $3,000 investment required by most funds.

Another Teenvestor-friendly fund, in terms of small investment requirements, is the USAA First Start Growth Fund, which also makes it possible for young people to invest small amounts of money on a regular basis. This fund's monthly investment requirement is $20—well within the range of a lot of Teenvestors.

While it is true that Teenvestors can probably find index funds or other funds that will earn higher returns than these Teenvestor-friendly funds, the Young Investor and First Start Growth funds offer something more to Teenvestors—educational materials for young investors.

Getting Information On Funds

The best way to begin investigating an index fund (indeed, any fund whatsoever) is to use the Internet for more information on the funds. We find the Microsoft Money Central, Smart Money, and the Morningstar sites, among others, to be particularly helpful in gathering information on specific mutual funds. Like stocks, mutual funds also have their own symbols so you can look them up easily in websites that specialize in mutual fund data.

ASSIGNMENT 15.1

Please find the symbols for the Vanguard 500 Index, the T. Rowe Price Total Equity Index 500, the USAA S&P 500 Index, and the Fidelity Spartan 500. In addition, list the current asset balances and the current NAVs for each mutual fund. On our website, you will find instructions on how to find information on any mutual fund and how to contact funds for their prospectuses.

Costs Of Investing In A Mutual Fund

When you buy a mutual fund, you have to pay an up-front fee for the privilege of buying the fund, and you have to pay an ongoing fee for as long as you own the fund. You can find the estimate for a fund's fees in the *fee table* near the front of the fund's prospectus.

You can use the fee table to compare the costs of different funds. The fee table breaks costs into two main categories: *sales loads* (paid when you buy, sell, or exchange your shares) and *expense ratios* (or yearly ongoing expenses).

Sales Loads

A *sales load* is a term you should become familiar with if you intend to invest in mutual funds. A sales load charged by a mutual fund is used to pay commissions to the people who sell the fund's shares to investors, as well as to pay for other marketing costs. Loads, which are usually given in percentage terms, can be as high as 6% of your investment. That is, if you invest $100 into buying a share of a mutual fund, $6 will be taken out to pay commission.

Some funds require you to pay the load when you buy shares of the fund. This is known as paying a *front-end load*. Others require that you pay when you sell your shares. This is known as paying a *back-end load*. Some funds charge no loads at all and these funds are known as *no-load funds*.

Of course, the bad thing about a front-end load is that it eats your money away immediately as soon as you invest in the fund. This may not be so bad if the value of your investment is going to sky-rocket. We recommend that Teenvestors stick only to funds that have no loads associated with them.

Expense Ratio

Regardless as to whether a fund has a load or not, funds charge investors each year primarily for managing the investments in the fund. Remember that in a mutual fund you leave the responsibility of determining what stocks to invest in to the people managing the fund. The fund manager makes buy and sell decisions for stocks in the fund and, of course, the manager is paid handsomely for his or her efforts each month. The cost of running the fund also includes such things as basic as printing and postage expenses associated with the statements mailed to fund owners. Finally, funds also charge investors what's known as *12b-1 fees*—marketing and distribution fees. All of these costs are lumped into what is called the *expense ratio*—the percentage of the value of your investment that will go towards paying these costs for each year that the investor owns the fund.

Some investors mistakenly believe that if the expense ratios of their funds are high, it must mean that the managers of the funds are really good. The truth is that funds with high expense ratios do not typically perform better than funds with low expense. But there may be circumstances in which you decide it is appropriate for you to pay higher expenses. For example, you can expect to pay higher expenses for certain types of funds that require extra work by its managers, such as international stock funds, which require more sophisticated research. You may also pay higher expenses for funds that provide special services, like toll-free telephone numbers, check-writing and automatic investment programs.

A difference in expenses that may look small to you can make a big difference in the value of your investment over time. In other words, the higher the expense ratio, the lower your return will be especially if you hang on to a mutual fund for a long time.

With regard to expense ratios, we recommend that, before you buy a mutual fund, you find out from the prospectus the estimates for the expenses that will be charged by the fund. The prospectus should lay all these expenses out in detail for you.

ASSIGNMENT 15.2

Look up the following information about the Vanguard 500 Index funds: the asset balance of the fund, its investment goal, and the return of the fund's assets for each of the past 5 years.

TAXES

You may owe taxes on any year you receive or reinvest distributions from your mutual fund. You may also owe taxes on any capital gains you receive when you sell your shares. Just as with stocks, you have to *k*eep your account statements in order to figure out your taxes at the end of the year. If you invest in a *tax-exempt fund* (such as a municipal bond fund), some or all of your dividends will be exempt from federal (and sometimes state and local) income tax. You may, however, owe taxes on any capital gains.

Our website, www.teenvestor.com, will point you to a few great sites for more information about mutual funds.

16

BUYING STOCKS DIRECTLY FROM COMPANIES

Did you know that you could buy stock directly from public companies without going through a broker? In this chapter, you will learn about the two ways public companies allow you to buy their stock directly from them: through direct purchase plans and dividend reinvestment plans (DRIPS). You will learn how these plans work, the major difference between the two, and how to use these investment plans effectively so you can get the most for your investment dollar.

WHY COMPANIES OFFER DIRECT PURCHASE PLANS AND DRIPS

You may be wondering why companies would want to encourage small-time investors to buy their stock by offering direct purchase plans and DRIPS. The answer is quite simple—companies that offer some form of stock purchase plans see them as a way to encourage an investor to become a loyal customer. For example, if you own shares in McDonald's, chances are that you would rather buy McDonald's food than Burger King's (assuming you occasionally eat fast food). In addition, direct purchase plans give companies a cheap way to raise money directly from investors rather than going through investment bankers who would underwrite stock offerings.

THE DIFFERENCE BETWEEN DIRECT PURCHASE PLANS AND DRIPS

The companies that have some form of a stock purchase programs now number over 1,000. As mentioned earlier, stock purchase programs come in two varieties: direct purchase plans and dividend reinvestment plans (DRIPS).

Direct Purchase plans

Companies that allow you *to purchase your first share*, and all other shares, of their stock directly from them without going through a broker are said to have direct purchase plans. These shares are also called *no-load-stock* or *no-load-shares* because you can purchase them without a broker's fee or *load* (although you may be charged a small administrative fee).

Although the companies that offer direct purchase plans are few (numbering in the hundreds), there are more and more each year.

A number of companies that you have probably heard of like McDonald's, Mattel, Exxon, Home Depot, Gillette, International Business Machines (IBM), J.C. Penny Company, Procter & Gamble Company, Sears, Roebuck & Company, Texaco, Inc., and Wal-Mart all offer direct purchase plans.

Dividend Reinvestment Plans (DRIPS)

Companies that allow you to buy additional shares of their stock directly from them *only if you already own one or more shares of the company's stock* are said to have dividend reinvestment plans (DRIPS).

You will find that some investors use the terms "direct purchase plans" and "DRIPS" interchangeably but there really is a difference between the two. This difference can be significant to Teenvestors, who have little money to invest in the first place. The only, but important, difference between direct purchase plans and DRIPS is that a company that offers only DRIPS will not allow you to purchase your first share from it directly. Unless you already own a share of that company and it is registered in your name, you would have to purchase your first share of the company's stock through a broker. Of course, once you have that initial share, you're set. You can then participate in the DRIP program and take advantage of the reduced fees offered through the program. Companies such as PepsiCo, General Electric, and Exxon, have their own dividend reinvestment plans or DRIPS. The "dividend reinvestment" part of these plans refers to the fact that when you participate in them, your dividends are automatically reinvested in additional shares of the company's stock.

THE STOCK REGISTRATION REQUIREMENT

Both direct purchase plans and DRIPS require that all shares you buy as a participant in the plans be registered in your name. Usually, when a stockbroker buys shares for you, the stocks are registered in the name of the firm for which the broker works (or in the *street name*, as it is called). For example, if you buy one share of Nike's stock through a broker, the share belongs to you but Nike does not have any idea that you actually own it. All Nike knows is that your broker has one share that belongs to someone. To participate in DRIPS, however, the company whose stock you own must be aware that you, in fact, do own one of their shares. The way this is accomplished is that if you go through a broker to buy your initial share, you must have him or her register the security in your name and have the stock certificate mailed to you. The certificate is the proof that companies with stock investment plans need in order to allow you to participate in their programs.

Some brokerage firms charge a fee of $15 to $25 for transferring the security in your name. Others charge more affordable fees for this transfer. After the transfer, the company whose stock you own will recognize you as a shareholder and it will send annual reports and other investment material directly to you. More importantly, you will then qualify for the company's DRIP plan if it has one.

ADVANTAGES OF DIRECT PURCHASE PLANS AND DRIPS

In general, the major advantages of direct purchase plans and DRIPS are as follows:

1. *Both Encourage Teenvestors To Get Into The Market.* When a Teenvestor finds a good, stable company with strong growth potential, she can start a small portfolio and build it over time. Take Exxon Mobil for instance. The company requires that you make an initial investment of $250 in its DRIP plan before you can purchase additional shares. Another company, Heinz, requires an initial investment of the value of one share. On the higher end of the

initial investment scale, McDonald's has a much higher minimum initial investment amount of $1,000.

2. *Both Charge Very Little In Brokerage Fees.* The companies save investors brokerage fees by pooling the money of the various investors before approaching brokers who will buy the shares. This way, the fees are effectively reduced for each investor.

3. *Both Allow Optional Cash Investments*—that is, they allow you to buy additional shares periodically. While the initial investment amount for Exxon Mobil Oil is $250, the additional monthly investment is $50. For Heinz, which has an initial investment requirement of one share, the additional required monthly investment is $25. McDonald's has a minimum initial investment of $1,000 and a monthly-required investment of $100. While some companies establish minimums and maximums of additional periodic purchases you can make, many plans allow the investor to contribute as little as $10 or $25 to the plan for the purchase of more shares. What this means is that for some investment plans, a Teenvestor can buy fractions of a share. For example, if the stock price of a company offering a DRIP is $100 but you have only $10, you can actually invest that $10 in that DRIP and buy 1/10th of a share (1/10 = $10/$100).

4. *Both Plans Permit Dividend Reinvestment.* This is great for Teenvestors because the dividends they will be getting on just a few shares of stock would not amount to much. It is, therefore, better to just keep it all in the till to buy additional shares.

DISADVANTAGES OF DIRECT PURCHASE PLANS AND DRIPS

You can buy all your shares of a company that has a Direct Purchase Plan from that company. However, for a company with DRIPS, you must already own at least one share of the company's stock before you can buy additional shares through its DRIP program. Of course this means that if you want to join a company's DRIP program, you will have to get your hands on at least one share of that company's stock. It can be expensive to buy just one share of stock, but it is getting cheaper every day because of the ability to buy shares online. We will discuss online brokers more in Chapter 20.

Another disadvantage, as we mentioned earlier, is that even if you are able to buy one share of stock so you can invest in a DRIP program, you still have to have the stock issued in your name, and not the "street name." A broker (online or not) will often charge you to make this name transfer.

Taxes are another disadvantage of direct purchase plans and DRIPS. Since you can invest monthly in these plans, you have to be organized enough to keep accurate records about the amount and the timing of your purchases and of your reinvested dividends. We won't go through the specifics of the tax issues here, but you should understand that the greater the variety of stocks you own in these plans, the more complicated the tax calculations can become.

Finally, another disadvantage of direct purchase plans and DRIPS is that they are not for people who want to invest in a company's stock for a short period of time like a year or two. These plans are for long-term investors—people who want to invest for at least 5 years. This is not really a disadvantage for Teenvestors since their investment goals should be for investment gains over the long-term. If you do your research, you are likely to find companies whose stock prices will grow over the long-term.

ASSIGNMENT 16.1

Find out which of the 30 companies in The Dow have either direct purchase plans or dividend reinvestment plans. See our website for how to complete the assignment if you don't already know how to do so.

TRENDS IN DIRECT INVESTMENTS

Recall that the advantages of direct purchase plans and DRIPS include the fact that Teenvestors can (1) avoid big brokerage commissions by buying shares directly from companies, (2) invest small amounts regularly, and (3) buy fractions of shares.

A handful of online brokers are now offering some of the same advantages as these plans and much more. Specifically, they (1) charge as little as $3 for each transaction, (2) require minimum investment balances as low as $20 for their list of eligible stocks (which range from 1,000 to 2,000 stocks), (3) allow investors to buy fractions of a share, and (4) keep records of transactions (which eliminates a big investment headache). Buyandhold Inc, and Share builder are the most prominent of these types of online companies that provide the benefits of direct purchase plans and DRIPS without some of the hassles. Some of these online companies, however, require that they withdraw money for stock purchases directly from their customers' checking accounts. This could be a problem for many Teenvestors who can't maintain large enough balances in their checking accounts to justify keeping them open. We hope that your parents can help you come up with creative ways to solve this problem if you intend to use these low-cost online brokers.

On our website, www.teenvestor.com, you will find more information about direct purchase plans and DRIPS.

17

OTHER INVESTMENTS

Even though the stock market is the best place to invest your money, there are a few other financial assets you can buy. Certificates of Deposit, U.S. Savings Bonds, and Zero Coupon Bonds are just a few examples of other investments Teenvestors can afford with their small budgets. These three financial assets all behave like bonds because they all pay interest on invested amounts that are typically higher than any interest you will get in a regular savings account in a bank.

CERTIFICATES OF DEPOSITS

Certificates of deposit or CDs as they are commonly known, are small loans investors make to banks for a few months to several years. The amount of money loaned is usually called the *principal* of the loan. The amount of time for which the loan is made is usually known as the *maturity* or *term* of the loan.

CDs are insured by a government insurance agency called the Federal Deposit Insurance Corporation. The minimum investment balance is usually a few hundred dollars and can be as high as several hundred thousand dollars. Needless to say, the interest rates you will receive on CDs are small—usually in the 4% to 7% range, depending on the level of inflation and the condition of the economy in general. When CDs mature (i.e. the bank has to give you back your principal), you usually have the option of reinvesting in other CDs. Ask your parents about purchasing CDs in the bank they use for their own finances.

U.S. SAVINGS BONDS

Savings Bonds are loans American citizens make to the government. The Series EE U.S. Savings Bonds (or Series EE Bonds) accumulate interest, which is paid only when you cash the bond in. You can buy these bonds from any bank and other financial institutions. The way Series EE Bonds work is that you are promised a certain amount of money when they mature or when you sell them. The amount you get when they mature is called the "face value" of the bond. Series EE U.S. Savings Bonds are sold in face value amounts of $50, $75, $100, $200, $500, $1,000, $5,000, and $10,000. What you pay to buy the bond is half the face value. For example, if the face value is $100, you pay only $50 to buy the Series EE Bond. The bond accumulates interest (currently around 5%), which is not distributed to you until the bond matures, or you sell it (which you can do six months after you buy it). The bond matures when it has accumulated interest that is equal to the amount of money you paid for the bond.

ZERO COUPON BONDS

Zero coupon bonds behave just like U.S. Savings Bonds except that corporations and the government can issue them as well. An investment in a zero coupon bond, however, will cost you a lot more up-front cash—perhaps in the thousands. Not many Teenvestors will be able to afford this investment but it is an option nevertheless. Some online brokers will be able to sell you zero coupon bonds.

> On our website, www.teenvestor.com, you will find more information on U.S. Savings Bonds and how to purchase them online. In addition, the site will give you information about other appropriate investments for Teenvestors, as we learn about them.

18

THE RIGHT TIME AND THE RIGHT WAY TO INVEST

Before you can start investing, you have to accumulate enough money or know that you will be getting money in your hands on a regular basis. In addition, you must be able to discipline yourself to invest on a regular basis for a long period of time. In this chapter, we will discuss when and how to start investing.

WHEN TO START INVESTING

So, you have identified some stocks and mutual funds in which to invest. What do you do next? If you are putting aside a certain amount of money each month in anticipation of making investments in stocks or in mutual funds, we recommend that you accumulate at least $50 to $100 each time you want to invest. For mutual funds, you may have no choice anyway because many of them require that you invest in $100 chunks. For stocks, investing less than $50 is a waste of money because the investment fees you will be charged by some brokers (as we will discuss later) can be $10 or more each time you buy shares. This will eat into your actual investment amount if you buy stocks frequently. It is probably a good idea to alert some of your relatives—grandparents, uncles, aunts, and others—to the fact that you invest in chunks of $50 to $100 periodically in stocks and mutual funds so they can appropriately time and bundle their cash gifts to you.

HOW TO START INVESTING

For people with little money, it is better to choose one or two stocks and invest in them regularly and hold on to them for a long, long time. The following sections discuss the process of a periodic investment strategy called *dollar cost averaging*.

Dollar Cost Averaging

You could make lots of money in the stock market if you knew exactly when the price of a stock will hit its low point, and when it will hit its high point. You simply buy at the low point, and sell at the high point. Sounds easy, right? The truth is that no one can really tell you for sure when prices will move up and down. The only thing that anyone can say is that over a very long period of time, stock prices tend to go up. But even though stock prices go up in the long run, there are periods when there are downturns in the market. Stock prices, therefore, have their own unpredictable rhythms.

Because predicting the movement of stock prices is virtually impossible, it is best to ignore the market and invest steadily by using the dollar cost averaging approach to investing. Dollar cost averaging is the method of investment whereby the same amount of money is invested periodically in a stock (or in another financial asset like a mutual fund) regardless of its price. Some investors use this method because it takes the guesswork out of investing. The technique works because of the fact that stock prices tend to go up in the long run. The following section, written for the advanced Teenvestor, goes into more details about how the dollar cost averaging investment technique works.

More On Dollar Cost Averaging
(For The Advanced Teenvestor)

The main point about dollar cost averaging is to invest regularly. The investment period could be once a month, once every two months, or in any given regular time period. Here is how it works.

Suppose you intend to invest $200 every three months to buy as many shares of a company's stock as you can over a period of one year. In that one-year period, you will invest $200 four times, or a total of $800. Suppose also that the prices of a share during the times when you want to make your purchase are as follows: $10, $8, $10, and $12. With this pattern of prices, you will be able to buy the following number of shares (rounded to the nearest whole number):

20 shares calculated as follows: $200 / $10
25 shares calculated as follows: $200 / $8
20 shares calculated as follows: $200 / $10
17 shares calculated as follows: $200 / $12

By the end of the one-year period, you would have purchased a total of 82 shares worth $984 calculated as follows:

82 shares x $12 per share = $984

Now suppose that you hadn't followed the dollar cost averaging technique. If you spent the entire $800 at the beginning of the period, you would have been able to purchase 80 shares (80 = $800/$10). If you spent the entire amount at the end of the period, you would have been able to purchase only about 67 shares ($800/$12). Dollar cost averaging allowed you to purchase 82 shares—more shares than investing the entire amount at the beginning or at the end of the period.

Dollar cost averaging works only when stock prices go up in the long run. If for example, the stock prices for the four times you wanted to invest the $200 were $10, $8, $8, and $7, you would have ended up with 99 shares worth $693 ($693 = 99 shares x $7 per share), which is a difference of $107 ($107 = $800 - $693).

Just remember that you may have to hang on to your investments for years before dollar cost averaging pays off.

WHY OUR INVESTMENT STRATEGY WORKS

Investing regularly no matter what is happening in the stock market (or with any other financial assets) works because of the fact that in the long run, stock prices tend to go up. This is in line with our statement earlier in the book that in the past 72 years, the stock market has earned a return of over 11% per year for investors. To appreciate the importance of investing in a financial asset like a stock over a long period of time, you have to understand the effect of compounding. We discussed compounding at length in Chapter 10 but it is worth reviewing again.

Compounding is the multiplying effect of investing money in a financial asset over a long period of time. To give you an example of how compounding works, let's see what happens if you deposit

$1,000 in a bank account which pays you 10% interest each year. At the end of the first year, your interest is calculated as follows:

$$\$1,000 \times 10\% = \$100$$

At the end of the first year, the new amount you will have in the bank (if you keep all your money with the bank) will increase by the $100 interest you earned at the end of the year to $1,100. At the end of the second year, you will earn 10% interest again, but this time the interest will be based on the new balance of $1,100 and will be calculated as follows:

$$\$1,100 \times 10\% = \$110$$

At the end of the second year, the new amount you will have in the bank will increase by the $110 interest you earned at the end of the second year to $1,210.

If you keep your money in the bank and earn the interest each year over a long period of time, the money you would have will multiply because you will be earning interest on top of the interest you earned in previous years. Table 18.1, at the end of this chapter, shows how much an initial deposit of $1,000 in a bank account grows if the interest compounds at 5%, 10% and 15% annually. Notice how the amount of money in the account grows by leaps and bounds depending on the interest rate. In the 50th year after depositing just $1,000 in the account, the money grows to $11,467 if the interest rate is 5%, $117,391 if the interest rate is 10% and $1,083,657 if the interest rate is 15%. The compounding effect is found with any investment, not just a bank deposit, in which you earn a certain return (which is really just like earning interest).

You are probably saying to yourself that you can't even see yourself 50 years from now. Just remember that whether it is 5 years, 10 years, 20 years or 50 years, you are better off letting your money grow by keeping it in one place for a long time and letting compounding work for you. In addition, the compounding example we gave above assumed you invested (that is, you put in a bank) $1,000 just one time. Imagine what could happen if you made this investment once a year, year after year, for 50 years. If you invested $1,000 per year for 50 years, you would have $219,865 (at 5% per year interest), $1,280,349 (at 10% per year interest) or $8,300,424 (at 15% per year interest) at the end of 50 years. Even if you invest just $1,000 per year for only 10 years, you will have $13,217 (at 5% per year interest), $17,541 (at 10% per year interest) and $23,359 (at 15% per year interest). No matter how you slice it, steady investment over a long period of time is your best bet to put away money for your future.

TABLE 18.1
A One-Time Investment Of $1,000

Years	Yearly 5%	Compounding 10%	Rates 15%
1	$ 1,050	$ 1,100	$ 1,150
2	$ 1,103	$ 1,210	$ 1,323
3	$ 1,158	$ 1,331	$ 1,521
4	$ 1,216	$ 1,464	$ 1,749
5	$ 1,276	$ 1,611	$ 2,011
6	$ 1,340	$ 1,772	$ 2,313
7	$ 1,407	$ 1,949	$ 2,660
8	$ 1,477	$ 2,144	$ 3,059
9	$ 1,551	$ 2,358	$ 3,518
10	$ 1,629	$ 2,594	$ 4,046
11	$ 1,710	$ 2,853	$ 4,652
12	$ 1,796	$ 3,138	$ 5,350
13	$ 1,006	$ 3,452	$ 6,153
14	$ 1,980	$ 3,797	$ 7,076
15	$ 2,079	$ 4,177	$ 8,137
16	$ 2,183	$ 4,595	$ 9,358
17	$ 2,292	$ 5,054	$ 10,761
18	$ 2,407	$ 5,560	$ 12,375
19	$ 2,527	$ 6,116	$ 14,232
20	$ 2,653	$ 6,727	$ 16,367
21	$ 2,786	$ 7,400	$ 18,822
22	$ 2,925	$ 8,140	$ 21,645
23	$ 3,072	$ 8,954	$ 24,891
24	$ 3,225	$ 9,850	$ 28,625
25	$ 3,386	$ 10,835	$ 32,919
26	$ 3,556	$ 11,918	$ 37,857
27	$ 3,733	$ 13,110	$ 43,535
28	$ 3,920	$ 14,421	$ 50,066
29	$ 4,116	$ 15,863	$ 57,575
30	$ 4,322	$ 17,449	$ 66,212
31	$ 4,538	$ 19,194	$ 76,144
32	$ 4,765	$ 21,114	$ 87,565
33	$ 5,003	$ 23,225	$ 100,700
34	$ 5,253	$ 25,548	$ 115,805
35	$ 5,516	$ 28,102	$ 133,176
36	$ 5,792	$ 30,913	$ 153,152
37	$ 6,081	$ 34,004	$ 176,125
38	$ 6,385	$ 37,404	$ 202,543
39	$ 6,705	$ 41,145	$ 232,925
40	$ 7,040	$ 45,259	$ 267,864
41	$ 7,392	$ 49,785	$ 308,043
42	$ 7,762	$ 54,764	$ 354,250
43	$ 8,150	$ 60,240	$ 407,387
44	$ 8,557	$ 66,264	$ 468,495
45	$ 8,985	$ 72,890	$ 538,769
46	$ 9,434	$ 80,180	$ 619,585
47	$ 9,906	$ 88,197	$ 712,522
48	$ 10,401	$ 97,017	$ 819,401
49	$ 10,921	$ 106,719	$ 942,311
50	**$ 11,467**	**$ 117,391**	**$ 1,083,657**

On our website, www.teenvestor.com, you will find more information on the right time and the right way to invest.

19

THE LAW, TAXES AND RECORDS

There are three important aspects of investing that Teenvestors should be aware of—the law regarding young investors, the taxes on investment profits, and the role good record keeping plays in investing.

THE LAW

Minors are not allowed to own stocks, mutual funds, and other financial assets outright. In some states, minors are defined as young people less than 18 years old and in others they are defined as young people less than 21 years old.

As a minor, you can make investments only under the supervision of your parent through a *custodial account*. One of your parents will have to sign you up for the custodial account. You own the assets in the account but your parents control the investments in it (hopefully, with your help). According to the law, even though the investments in the account belong to you, you can't sell the investments or do anything on your own as it relates to the account until you are no longer a minor. This means that if your state considers you an adult at age 18, you can do whatever you want with the investments in the account at that age.

TAXES

The tax law is quite favorable when it comes to custodial accounts. The Internal Revenue Service (IRS) calls the combination of the following items *unearned income* or *investment income*: interest, dividends and capital gains. The tax laws say that if your parents open up a custodial account for you, you can make up to $700 of investment income before you have to pay taxes. We have explained all the details to your parents in the next chapter. Read it if you are brave enough, but your parents will probably have to explain some of it to you. Chances are pretty good that you won't have to pay any taxes or fill out any tax forms because your investments will probably be very small, at least in the beginning.

The math involved in calculating tax is simple. If you have to pay tax on any amount, the tax is determine as follows:

Tax = (Tax Rate) x (Amount Being Taxed)

Where Tax Rate is in percentage terms (such as 15%, etc.)

If you want to know the amount you actually keep after paying taxes, the formula is as follows:

After-Tax Amount You Keep = (1 – Tax Rate) x (Amount Being Taxed)

Regardless of the current size of your investments, you should keep good records because your investments may grow to the point where you will have to pay the IRS. In addition, when you keep good records, you will know exactly how much money you are making in specific investments.

RECORD KEEPING

Keeping accurate and up–to–date business records is, for many Teenvestors, the most difficult and uninteresting aspect of investing. Proper record-keeping is important for several reasons. For one thing, the U.S. government wants its share of the money you make by investing in stocks, mutual funds and other investments. It is likely that you won't have to file taxes because you probably won't make that much money on your investments. However, a well-designed record-keeping system from the very beginning will help you avoid problems just in case you end up doing really well and have to pay taxes in future years.

In addition, a simple, well-organized system of records, regularly kept up, can actually be a time-saver because it can help you figure out exactly how much money you are truly making on your individual investments. For example, when you buy stocks from an online broker, you should record how much you paid for them as well as the *transaction costs* or *commissions* associated with the purchases. The transaction cost is the commission an online broker charges you to buy or sell an investment. If you don't record your transaction costs, you could end up thinking that you made more money than you actually did. Consider the scenario in the following paragraph.

You buy 4 shares of XYZ stock at the beginning of the year for $30 each, and your online broker charges you $5 to buy the shares and $5 to sell the shares. The amount of money you give the online broker for buying the shares is $120 before considering the $5 transaction cost associated with the purchase. At the end of the year, the share price for XYZ stock has gone up to $40 per share so you will receive $160 for the sale of the shares before considering the $5 transaction cost associated with the sale. The simplified before-tax return on investment can be calculated as follows:

Return On Investment = (Ending Value - Beginning Value - Transaction Costs) / Beginning Value

Return On Investment = ($160 - $120 - $5 - $5) / $120 = .25 = 25%

Thus, your true return was 25% for the year. If you had not accounted for your transaction costs, which totaled $10, you might have calculated your return as follows:

($160 - $120) / $120 = .33 = 33%

By not considering your transaction costs, you would have thought that you made a 33% return on the money you invested instead of the true return of 25%. If you make this kind of mistake, you could end up paying higher taxes than you actually owe.

Another situation where proper record-keeping is important is with capital gains—the profit you make, if any, when you sell a share of stock, mutual funds, and other assets after subtracting your transaction costs. The simplified version of the calculation is as follows:

Capital Gains = (Ending Value - Beginning Value - Transaction Costs)

The calculation in the equation above can be positive or negative. A negative capital gain is another way of saying that you have a *capital loss*—in other words, you lost money on your investment. We won't deal with the case where you have a capital loss here because we hope

that when you sell your stocks or mutual funds, you are doing so because you will have positive capital gains.

The amount of tax you owe on your capital gains will depend on
how long you have held on to that stock. The longer you hold the stock
(and other assets), the less the IRS taxes you on capital gains made on
the stock. The IRS recognizes three holding periods for capital gains:
one for stocks held for one year or less, another for stocks held for
greater than a year but less than 5 years, and another for stocks held for
more than 5 years. Capital gains on stocks held for less than one year
are taxed at your normal tax rate (we assume, 10% or 15%). Capital
gains on stocks held for over a year but less than 5 years are taxed at
10%. Capital gains on stocks held for more than 5 years are taxed at
8%. As you can see, in order to apply these two separate tax rates on
capital gains, you have to keep proper records on the price of each stock,
the date on which you bought the stock, the transaction costs or commissions, and so on.

Your record-keeping task is made somewhat easier because you
will probably not have a big portfolio of investments. Make three copies
of the Worksheet 19.1, on the next page, to record your stock, mutual
fund, and direct stock purchase transactions.

Worksheet 19.1
Record-Keeping Spreadsheet

Name Of Stock/Fund	Date Of Purchase Or Sale	Number Of Shares	Purchase Or Sale Price	Commission Paid To Broker, etc.

On our website, www.teenvestor.com, you will find more information on taxes and on record-keeping.

20

ONLINE BROKERS

It used to be that you could buy shares of companies only through a handful of companies called *full-service brokers*. These brokers could buy and sell shares for customers but they charged big fees for each transaction, especially if you bought less than 100 shares (or a *round lot* as it is known) of any given stock. For example, you could end up paying up to $100 just to buy 20 shares of a company's stock. These types of brokers claimed that they charged their customers so much for the stock transactions because they provided them with good research information. In truth, customers really had no choice but to use these brokers. Investors either had to invest in stocks through the full-service brokers or keep their money out of the stock market entirely.

Gradually, things began to change. The government made it easier for the existence of *discount brokers*—companies that helped investors buy and sell shares at a much lower price than the full-service brokers (although discount brokers provided very little research on companies). But even though discount brokers slashed the cost of buying and selling shares by half or more, they were still relatively costly—especially for the beginning Teenvestor.

In the past few years, however, the cost of investing has gone down dramatically because of *online brokers*—companies that can sell or buy shares for you through the Internet with costs as low as $3 for each transaction. Online brokers like Etrade, Datek, Ameritrade, and many others have helped revolutionize the way America buys and sells stocks. They did this so well that a big full-service broker like Merrill Lynch finally decided to allow its customers to buy and sell stocks online because it was concerned about losing business to online brokers.

The full-service brokers had always boasted that they provided investors with research and advise on companies in which they were interested in investing. Their research and advice is especially helpful for the beginning investor who has no clue about which of the thousands of companies out there she should invest in. But even that advantage is quickly going away because the Internet is full of free research and financial information that can help investors decide what stocks to buy or sell. And for a small fee, investors can get some of the best research on Wall Street.

While online brokers are plentiful on the Internet, it can be quite confusing to sift through all the sites in order to determine which broker best suits your needs. In this chapter, we have drawn up some simple guidelines to help you and your parents decide which broker to use. Just as a reminder, you can't buy and sell stocks unless your parents open a custodial account on your behalf. If you are 18 years old or older, you can open up your own individual account on your own in most states.

HOW TO CHOOSE A TEENVESTOR-FRIENDLY ONLINE BROKER

One of the first investment decisions you and your parents will have to make, after you decide on companies in which to invest, is what broker to use. Your parents must be involved in this decision because they will have to fill out the custodial account application you need before you can buy stocks or mutual funds through an online broker. They can also help you understand the pros and cons of going with specific brokers. Here are our suggestions about the important considerations when choosing an online broker.

Broker Insurance

Before you can even begin to look at the features offered by an online broker, you should find out if the broker is insured. The government-sponsored Securities Investor Protection Corporation (SIPC) will cover investments made with reputable brokers. The SIPC insures accounts up to $100,000 in cash. This insurance covers you if your broker goes bankrupt. It doesn't cover you for making poor investment decisions. If a broker is not SIPC insured, you shouldn't invest through that broker under any circumstances.

Minimum Balances

Of course, most Teenvestors are short on cash so they need online brokers that require little or no minimum balance in a trading account before he can begin buying stocks. Some of the biggest online brokers that you see being advertised on television (such as Etrade, Datek and Ameritrade) require minimum trading account balances of $500 to $2,000. But there are other reputable companies such as Quick & Reilly and Firstrade that have no minimum balance to open up trading accounts. You will find though, that in some cases, the lower the minimum balance required, the higher the cost per trade.

Low Trading Cost

Trading costs are going down every day. Companies like BuyandHold and ShareBuilder now charge $3 (on top of the price of the shares you want to buy) to purchase stock for you. There is even a company, Freetrade.com (owned by Ameritrade), which is offering free trades. However, this online broker is not appropriate for Teenvestors because it has a minimum investing balance of $5,000 and other restrictions on accounts. All of this is good news for Teenvestors, and we hope (and believe) that trading costs will go down further for all reputable online brokers.

The only downside to some of these really inexpensive online brokers is that they don't offer as many investment options as full-service online brokers. For example, at the time of this writing, BuyandHold can buy and sell shares for you on only two occasions during the day. So, if the price of a stock is moving around a lot, you may, by the time the company gets around to buying the shares for you, end up paying more for the stock than the price you originally saw on your computer screen. However, this is not a big issue for beginning Teenvestors because they should not really be buying stocks whose prices fluctuates too much. In other words, they should not be buying stocks that are risky. Teenvestors should begin with big market-cap and low beta stocks when making purchases through special online brokers like BuyandHold. All in all, super-cheap online brokers, even though their services are very limited, are ideal for Teenvestors.

Low Trading Cost
(For The Advanced Teenvestor)

Another consideration when choosing an online broker is the cost to buy and sell shares. At the time of this writing, you can trade for as low as $5 for what is called a *market order*. A market order is an order to buy or sell stock at the currently available price. When you place a market order, you can't control the price at which your order will be filled. You simply get the price of the stock at the time the online broker executes your order.

In looking for a good online broker, you should not only be concerned with getting a low market order cost, but you should also be concerned about the cost of a *limit order*. A limit order is an order to buy or sell at a specific price. A buy limit order can be filled only at the limit price or lower, and a sell limit order can be filled only at the limit price or higher.

Typically, a market order will cost you less than a limit order. We have seen differences between the two of $2 to $5. We think that it is always worth it to go for limit orders wherever practical.

As an example of how a market order is better than a limit order, suppose that you want to buy the stock of company XYZ that has a current price of $20 per share. You know the price moves around a lot but you place a market order anyway. If the price jumps to $25 per share, a few seconds after you place your order, the online broker will buy the stock for you at $25 per share and deduct that money from your trading account. In this case, the stock will be purchased for $5 more than the price of $20 when you first placed your order ($25-$20 = $5). The way to protect yourself against this type of price increase is to place a limit order that is slightly above the current price so that you are not forced to buy the stock at a high price if the price jumps up dramatically. If you had set a limit buy order at $21 per share, the online broker would not have made a purchase until the share price was less than or equal to $21. Thus, the limit order is a ceiling on what you are willing to pay for the stock. Of course, there is a time limit on how long the limit order is open. It can be open for a day or until the price comes down to the limit order.

When you think about it, placing a limit order is not so important if the stock you are thinking about buying does not move around much. Most of the stocks in The Dow, for example, have pretty stable prices compared with some of the technology stocks in the NASDAQ Composite. We recommend that Teenvestors who are moving beyond investing in the biggest and safest companies (and moving toward mid-cap, small-cap, technology, and high beta stocks), place limit orders.

Hidden Costs

While a low minimum balance for opening a trading account and a low trading cost are desirable, watch out for hidden costs for other services for which you will be charged. The most common thing for some not-so-reputable brokers to do is to charge low commissions but add handling charges of, say, $5, to the commission.

One expense you may want to consider as well is the cost of transferring a stock certificate in your name. If you recall, in order to buy stock directly from direct purchase plans or from DRIP programs, you have to own at least one share of stock in your name (as described in Chapter 16). If you buy a share through your online broker and then want to buy additional shares directly from the company whose share you have purchased, your online broker must first transfer the certificate for the first share in your name. The charge for this transfer by some online brokers can be as high as $25.

There are other costs such as charges for making telephone inquiries about your account, getting duplicate statements, and other services for which some online brokers charge. If you ask for an investment package from the online broker, the package will outline all charges so you don't get any unpleasant surprises when you are billed $30 for a trade which you thought would cost only $8.

RECOMMENDATIONS ON WHAT BROKERS TO CONSIDER

We are always careful about mentioning specific online companies because sometimes the services and the fees of some of these companies change without notice. However, on our website you will find information about the companies that we consider to be truly Teenvestor-friendly. Each of these companies offers at least one of the following features:

1. Low or no minimum balance to open up accounts (as low as $0).

2. Low cost for trading (as low as $3).

3. Option to buy a fraction of a share. You can buy fractions of shares because you can just order a certain dollar amount of a stock. If, for example, a stock is worth $40 and you have only $20 to invest, you can buy half a share of that stock for $20.

4. Option to participate in Dividend Reinvestment Plans (DRIPS) without the usual hassle of keeping proper records for tax purposes.

On our website, www.teenvestor.com, you will find links to sites that provide lists of online brokers, complete with their trading costs, required minimum balances, and other important features you should consider when choosing a broker.

21

TAXES AND TAX-FRIENDLY INVESTMENTS (For Parents)

The tax issues associated with your Teenvestor's investments center around custodial accounts, IRAs and tuition savings plans. This chapter is not meant as a primer on how to calculate taxes on your Teenvestor's investment portfolio. It is simply a guide to highlight the tax consequences and benefits of the various investment options available to your Teenvestor.

At this juncture, we encourage you to purchase an investment tax guide and visit websites that thoroughly explain investment tax issues before you set up any of the accounts discussed in this chapter. Our website, www.teenvestor.com, will point you to some good tax books and investment websites. If the tax consequences of the custodial accounts, IRAs, and education plans are still not clear after reviewing these investment aids, we urge you to seek the advice of a financial advisor to ensure that there are no adverse tax consequences that would result from your Teenvestor's investment activities.

We must also caution you that as tax rates and tax thresholds change from time to time, some of the figures in this chapter may have changed by the time you read this book. You should get updates from the IRS or from our website.

CUSTODIAL ACCOUNTS

Custodial accounts provide your Teenvestor with a chance to purchase and sell securities under your supervision. These accounts are easy to establish and you can open them for your Teenvestor for stocks, mutual funds, direct stock investment plans, and other assets as long as he has a Social Security number.

A custodial account is held with an adult as the custodian but in the eyes of the law, the assets in the account belong to the child and are held in his name. The child, however, can't get his hands on the account's assets until he reaches his majority—18 years old in some states and 21 years old in others.

The custodian who establishes the account—typically a parent, grandparent or other relative—has management responsibility over the account. In other words, the custodian must be involved in all decisions to buy or sell securities or reinvest earnings generated by the account even though the investments in the account belong to a minor.

As we explain in more detail below, the beauty of establishing a custodial account is that the earnings and gains in the account are taxed at the owner's tax rate. This means that a Teenvestor for whom a custodial account has been established would pay taxes based on his own tax rate, which is generally less than the tax rate of a working adult.   For most Teenvestors, withdrawals or dividends associated with this account would be taxed at a rate of 10% or 15%.

Types of Custodial Accounts

There are two types of custodial accounts—the UGMA (named for the Uniform Gifts To Minors Act) and the UTMA (named for the Uniform Transfers To Minors Act). These two types of accounts are very similar in nearly all respects. The most significant difference between the two is the date at which control of the account passes to the child. A custodian loses control over an UGMA account once the child reaches his majority—18 or 21, depending upon the state. By contrast, a custodian is permitted to postpone transfer of control of an UTMA account to a child, depending upon the state, until 25.

Whether you establish an UTMA or an UGMA account, these accounts have very strict rules that prevent custodians from using them as their own personal piggybanks. Furthermore, while you can withdraw money from the account for your child's benefit, the assets in UGMA account can't be used as the source of cash to pay for things that you are legally obligated to provide to support your child (such as food, clothing, etc.). However, UTMA accounts are more liberal than UGMA in that they permit funds in the account to be spent for the support of the child.

Disadvantages of a Custodial Account

Criticisms of custodial accounts for children generally fall into three categories. First, even though you may have contributed to the balance in the custodial account in order to help your child get started as an investor, the assets belong to him. This means that if you wish to close the account and reclaim the assets, you may not only end up paying taxes at your own tax rate on the gains in the portfolio, but you may also find that the IRS will scrutinize your actions.

Second, custodial accounts raise thorny issues of "control." Some parents worry that their Teenvestor, upon reaching his majority, will squander the account's assets once he assumes control of the account.

Finally, substantial assets in custodial accounts can reduce a college-bound Teenvestor's eligibility for financial aid or cause tricky estate tax problems if the custodian dies before the child reaches his majority.

Advantages of a Custodial Account

Custodial accounts offer substantial advantages, which in our opinion outweigh the disadvantages discussed above. We believe that the most important advantage of a custodial account is that it enables your Teenvestor to learn how to invest responsibly, early in life, under your supervision. In addition, use of a custodial account will protect more of your Teenvestor's investment income than if he did not have such an account. This is because, as owner of the assets in the account, investment income generated by the account is taxed at his tax rate, which we assume, would be 10% or 15% in the case of most Teenvestors. As will be explained in detail below, this advantage is more limited for a child under 14 because investment income over $1,400 for such a child is taxed at the parent's tax rate, which is generally 27% or more. However, establishment of a custodial account is particularly beneficial for Teenvestors 14 years old and over because they are taxed at their own tax rate as compared to a parent's marginal tax rate.

We recommend that you keep the balance in the custodial account modest to ensure that concerns such as the adverse tax consequences associated with account closures, loss of custodial control over account assets, reduced financial aid or increased estate taxes no longer loom as large issues which stand in the way of the establishment of a custodial account for your Teenvestor.

FILING REQUIREMENTS AND TAX RATES

An in-depth discussion of the tax rules that apply to your Teenvestor's investment activities is certainly beyond the scope of this book. However, it's important that you know about the basic tax rules that govern when an income tax return must be filed for your Teenvestor and the appropriate income tax rate that will be applied to his income level.

Before covering some of the basic tax rules relevant to investing by Teenvestors, a brief discussion of the Economic Growth and Tax Reconciliation Act of 2001 (Tax Relief Act of 2001) is necessary. The Tax Relief Act of 2001 made a number of significant changes to the tax laws, including several areas of interest to you and your Teenvestor. Of particular interest are the provisions in the Act that:

- phase-in reductions in tax rates and create a new 10% tax bracket on the first $6,000 of income;
- increase the maximum contribution amounts for traditional and Roth IRAs; and

- increase and/or create new education tax-saving options that will help pay for primary, secondary, and higher education expenses for your Teenvestor.

In the following pages, we will discuss these new changes. However, it is important that you understand that the Tax Relief Act of 2001 contains a "sunset" provision. This provision states that after December 31, 2010, general tax brackets and the tax laws governing things like the Act's tax-deferred wealth accumulation opportunities (such as IRAs) may revert back to their 2001 levels. This reversion will take place unless Congress enacts a new law to extend the law beyond 2010.

One notable example to consider is the creation of the 10% tax bracket on the first $6,000 of income (for single filers) and the phase-in of tax reductions for the tax brackets over 15%. If, by the end of 2010, Congress has not enacted a new law, the 10% bracket disappears, leaving the 15% bracket as the lowest tax bracket. In addition, the phased-in tax bracket reductions will expire and taxpayers will see whopping increases in taxes as the rates revert back to the earlier rates prior to the enactment of the Tax Relief Act of 2001.

Since the Tax Relief Act of 2001 contains over 400 changes to the tax laws, it's likely that this and other changes may be of interest to you separate and apart from understanding the tax consequences of your Teenvestor's investment activity. Thus, we are sure that you will want to keep abreast of these developments to understand the potential consequences on your own taxes.

Recognizing When a Tax Return Must Be Filed

As a parent, you should monitor the amount of income that your Teenvestor receives. The IRS defines *investment income* (also known as *unearned income*) as the combination of interest, dividends and capital gains. Investment income should not be confused with *earned income*, which includes salaries, wages, taxable scholarships and grants.

In most instances, your Teenvestor, as a single dependent, will not be required to file or pay taxes on the first $700 of investment income (i.e., unearned income). However, once his investment income exceeds $700, he must file a tax return or, as discussed below, you may choose to include his investment income on your own tax return.

The rules discussed above apply to situations where your Teenvestor's only source of income is investment income. This income will be reported on his tax return and the amount owed will be calculated on Form 8615, which is to be attached to his return.

Parents can elect to include the investment income of their Teenvestors who are under 14 years of age on their own returns. Parents can make this election if their Teenvestor's investment income is more than $700 and less than $7,000. If you elect to report this income on your own tax return, your Teenvestor won't have to file a separate return. A parent's tax return, which includes the investment income of children under 14, must be accompanied with a completed Form 8814.

Gross income is used to determine whether your Teenvestor has to file a tax return when he has *both* investment income and earned income. Gross income, also known as "before-tax" income, is loosely defined as the total of earned income and investment income before any deductions for taxes are taken. Tax returns are required to be filed if your Teenvestor's gross income for the year is more than the larger of $700 or his earned income (up to $4,150) plus $250.

Generally, your Teenvestor will have to file a return if he has earned income (typically, wages from employment) that is greater than $4,400. This means that even if your Teenvestor doesn't have any investment income, a tax return must be filed if he earns more than $4,400 from a job. In addition, if your Teenvestor does not have any investment income and is self-employed—that is, if he is an entrepreneur—he will have to file a tax return if his net profit exceeds $400.

Determining the Appropriate Tax Bracket

Obviously, understanding when your Teenvestor is required to file a tax return is just one piece of the puzzle. It is also important to understand how to figure the tax rate that will be applied to his investment income.

Your Teenvestor is required to pay taxes on investment income over $700. The tax rate, which will be applied to this income, depends upon whether your Teenvestor is under 14 years of age or not. If he is under 14 years old and has investment income, he is subject to the *kiddie tax*. Technically speaking, the kiddie tax is not actually a tax but rather a restriction that seeks to prevent parents from transferring their investment assets to their children under 14 in order to shield their income from taxes.

Under the kiddie tax, investment income over $700 and up to $1,400 will be taxed at your Teenvestor's tax rate. For most Teenvestors, this rate would be at 10% or 15%. Any investment income over $1,400 will be taxed at the parent's tax rate.

When your Teenvestor turns 14, the kiddie tax rule no longer applies. Your Teenvestor is taxed at his own tax rate just like adults. It is still the case that he won't pay taxes on the first $700 of investment income. However, any investment income over $700 will be taxed at his tax rate, which is probably 10% or 15%.

INDIVIDUAL RETIREMENT ACCOUNTS (IRAs)

Another investment option available to Teenvestors is an Individual Retirement Account, or IRA. IRAs are tax-advantaged accounts that can be set up for retirement or educational purposes. They have a different set of restrictions from custodial accounts. In the sections below, we consider three different types of IRAs: the Roth IRA, the traditional IRAs, and Educational IRAs.

Socking money in an IRA for the "big payoff" at retirement five decades down the road is not going to motivate the average Teenvestor to invest in an IRA. The truth is that your Teenvestor will need a little incentive from you to get going with an IRA even though you may think that the only incentive he needs is that it's for his own good.

We'd like to suggest that you make the initial deposit in your Teenvestor's IRA account to get him started. You can also try a savings matching incentive program whereby you contribute more to an allowance, for example, if he conscientiously contributes money to the IRA from time to time. Do anything, including impounding a portion of cash gifts for relatives, to strongly encourage him to make contributions to an IRA, especially if he has no other investments.

Your Teenvestor may find it easier to maintain an IRA if he knows that one particular type of IRA, the Roth IRA, allows early withdrawals of contributions without a tax penalty as described in more detail below.

Roth IRAs

The *Roth IRA* has been increasingly popular since its enactment into law in 1997. An investor can make annual contributions with after-tax dollars to a Roth IRA account and accumulate earnings until age 59½, at which time he can withdraw the money tax-free. Your Teenvestor can establish a Roth IRA and buy stocks, bonds, and other assets for the account just like for a regular non-IRA custodial account.

Original *contributions* to a Roth IRA, as opposed to accumulated earnings (loosely coined, the profits generated by the account), can be withdrawn tax-free *prior* to age 59½ without a penalty, after five years. If however, your Teenvestor withdraws all his contributions, then proceeds to withdraw the accumulated earnings in the portfolio prior to turning 59½, he will not only pay taxes on the earnings but will also pay a 10% penalty as well. There are limited exceptions to this rule, including withdrawals for the purpose of paying qualified education expenses. See our website, www.teenvestor.com, for more details.

A Roth IRA, like any other IRA, can be set up through a bank or stockbroker. Many brokerage firms will open custodial IRAs for children. However, fees and minimum balances vary so it is necessary to shop around. To qualify as a Roth IRA, the account must be specifically designated as a Roth IRA. Contributions to the account must be made in the form of money (cash, check or money order) and that money can then be used to buy stocks, mutual funds, and other assets for the account.

A Teenvestor can have more than one type of IRA. However, the restriction is that his combined contribution to a Roth and Traditional IRA (as described in the next section) can't be greater than his total yearly wages and can't be greater than amount specified on Table 21.1.

TABLE 21.1

Contribution Amounts for Traditional and ROTH IRAs

Tax Year	Maximum Contribution Amount
2002	$3,000 annually
2003	$3,000 annually
2004	$3,000 annually
2005	$4,000 annually
2006	$4,000 annually
2007	$5,000 annually
2008	$5,000 annually
2009	Indexed (adjusted for inflation)

To reiterate, if your Teenvestor's taxable compensation is less than the maximum contribution amount allowable for the year, he may only contribute as much as he earns. However, if he earns more than that maximum contribution amount, he may only contribute the maximum contribution amount for the year.

Teenvestors can't contribute to their IRA in years in which they have no earned income. On the other hand, once the IRA is established, it is not necessary to contribute to it for every year in which income is earned. Contributing more than the amount allowable for the year to "make-up" for years in which little or no contribution was made is not permitted.

Anyone who works and thus receives earned income, or more specifically, taxable compensation (defined to include wages, salaries, tips, and amounts received for providing personal services), during the year can establish a Roth IRA.

The issue of what qualifies as earned income, for purposes of the Roth IRA, has generated a great deal of discussion in investment and tax circles. Everyone agrees that if a Teenvestor receives a W-2 form from a business (such as fast food restaurants, copy center, mall, etc.), this qualifies as proof of earned income for purposes of establishing a Roth IRA. But what about those situations where a Teenvestor does work around the neighborhood such as lawn mowing, or gets paid by his parents for work done in the home? These "jobs" do not generate a W-2. Some experts say that even in these situations, the Teenvestor *has* received "earned income" and *is* eligible to establish an IRA as long as the employee and the employer (parents, relatives, friends, neighbors, etc.) keep a record of the type of work performed, the number or hours worked, and the wages received. We suggest that you consult a tax professional and do more research on the matter if your Teenvestor has earned income that can't be substantiated by a W-2. The law is just not clear-cut in this area.

Both Roth and traditional IRAs (discussed below) have income limitations, which restrict higher wage earners from investing in them. It's unlikely that your Teenvestor needs to be concerned with these limitations because his earned income would probably not reach the income limitations. However, if you are concerned that your Teenvestor may be subject to these thresholds, we recommend that you consult IRS Publication 590 (*Individual Retirement Arrangements*), the IRS website (www.irs.gov), and a tax or investment consultant for more information.

Traditional IRAs

A *traditional IRA* allows your Teenvestor to make annual tax-deductible contributions. The contributions to the account are tax deferred until he reaches age 59½, at which point he can withdraw the money and get taxed at his tax rate at the time of the withdrawal. His tax rate at the time of the withdrawal at 59½ or later will probably be much lower than his tax rate during his working years. Your Teenvestor can buy stocks, bonds, and other assets with the money in the account just like a regular non-IRA custodial account or a Roth IRA.

Like Roth IRAs, your Teenvestor may only invest in a traditional IRA if he has earned income. This means that the traditional IRA raises the same "earned income" questions as discussed in the previous section concerning Roth IRAs. Traditional IRAs are also subject to the same contribution thresholds as Roth IRAs (see Table 21.1, above), and are set up the same way as Roth IRAs.

In general, contributions to traditional IRAs can't be withdrawn before age 59½ without a 10% penalty in addition to payment of regular income taxes. There are a limited number of exceptions to this rule, including withdrawals for the purpose of paying qualified education expenses.

There are two significant drawbacks to traditional IRAs. First, upon retirement, withdrawals from the IRA are taxed. As discussed above, with a Roth IRA, once the investor has reached age 59½, withdrawals from the account are tax-free. Second, contributions to traditional IRAs can't be withdrawn before age 59½ without a 10% penalty in addition to the payment of regular income taxes. There are a limited number of exceptions to this rule, including withdrawals for the purpose of paying qualified education expenses. By contrast, the Roth IRA permits withdrawal of original contributions prior to 59½ for any reason (after five years). For these reasons, many investment experts believe that the Roth IRA is superior to a traditional IRA, especially for young people with very little or no earned income.

Education IRAs

You can also help your Teenvestor open up an Education IRA that was established by Congress exclusively for the purpose of saving for higher education expenses on a tax-deferred basis. As a result of the enactment of the Tax Relief Act of 2001, Congress broadened this tax-saving option and opened it up as an investment vehicle to pay for public, private or religious school education for kindergarten through 12th grade as well. Qualifying higher education expenses include tuition, fees, books, supplies, equipment, and in the event that the Teenvestor is at least a half-time student, room and board. Under the Tax Relief Act of 2001, permitted elementary and secondary school expenses include: academic tutoring; specified computer technology expenses; and expenses for uniforms, transportation, and extended day programs. Education IRAs must be so designated at the time it is established. While your Teenvestor may have more than one

Education IRA, the total of all contributions to all Education IRAs can't exceed $2,000 per tax year, an increase as a result of the enactment of the Tax Relief Act from the prior $500 maximum contribution amount.

Education IRAs are similar to Roth IRAs in several ways. First, contributions to an Education IRA are not tax deductible. However, withdrawals are tax-free for payment of qualifying higher education expenses. Second, Education IRAs are subject to the same income limitations as Roth IRAs, which as we discussed earlier, need not be of concern for the average Teenvestor. Third, early withdrawals from Education IRAs are subject to the same 10% penalty rule for early withdrawals as traditional IRAs and Roth IRAs.

Unlike traditional IRAs and Roth IRAs, your Teenvestor can invest in an Education IRA whether or not he is employed. Contributions to an Educational IRA do not have to be combined with contributions to a traditional IRA or a Roth IRA. This means that your Teenvestor can invest $2,000 in an Education IRA while simultaneously contributing the maximum amount permitted to be contributed to traditional IRA and/or a Roth IRA for the year.

College Tuition Savings Plans

The primary drawback to the Education IRA is its $2,000 maximum contribution amount. By contrast, college tuition savings plans, also known as "529 Plans," with their higher contribution maximums, are considered to be superior investment vehicles to help parents and Teenvestors plan for college education. Under these plans, substantial contributions that are well above the Education IRA's $2,000 maximum contribution amount may be invested in a state-sponsored fund designed to help save for college tuition (and associated expenses such as room, board, books, and supplies). Most plans are open to both state residents and non-residents and the assets in the funds can be used to pay for education expenses at virtually any college in the country.

Prior to the enactment of the Tax Relief Act of 2001, the big advantage of these plans was that federal tax on the gains were deferred until the beneficiary entered college at which time the account's earnings were taxed at the student's rate as opposed to the typically higher rate of his parents. In most instances, this probably meant a federal tax rate of 10% or 15% since the beneficiary was a college student with little or no earned income. Now, with the passage of the Tax Relief Act of 2001, these plans have become even more valuable to college-bound Teenvestors. The distributions from these plans are no longer subject to tax from 2002 through 2010. Whether they will continue to be tax-free after the sunset date will depend upon whether Congress decides to extend the provision beyond 2010.

While the college tuition plans are excellent investment vehicles to pay for upcoming college expenses, they do have two drawbacks. First, when you put your money in these plans, you generally do not have control over how it is invested though some states are increasingly offering investors broader investment choices ranging from all equities to all bonds. However, once you have made the investment choice, it can't be changed. Second, if you contribute to a college plan in a given tax year, you can't make an Education IRA contribution in the same year for the same beneficiary. Despite these drawbacks, experts highly recommend these plans. Our site, www.teenvestor.com, will give you more information on these college savings plans. You can get information directly from The College Savings Plan Network's website, www.collegesavings.org.

MISCELLANEOUS TAX ISSUES ASSOCIATED WITH THE TYPICAL INVESTOR

At some point, many Teenvestors will receive cash or stock dividends or sell assets in their portfolios. In the event that your Teenvestor receives a dividend or sells assets in his account, a general understanding of the tax implications of the transaction would be helpful. For this reason, we include in this section a brief discussion of the basic tax rules applicable to cash dividends, stock dividends, capital gains and capital losses.

Cash or Stock Dividends

Corporations may elect to pay ordinary dividends to their shareholders, which are paid out of the earnings and profits of a corporation. While corporations can pay other types of dividends other than ordinary income, you can assume that any type of dividend that your Teenvestor receives on common or preferred stock is an ordinary dividend unless the paying corporation tells you otherwise. These dividends will be shown in box 1 of the Form 1099-DIV that you receive.

As we discussed in an earlier section, if your Teenvestor receives cash dividends, these dividends are treated as investment income. But what if he receives stock dividends? The general rule for stock dividends is that if your Teenvestor had no choice as to whether to receive either a cash or stock dividend, no income tax will be due on the stock dividend until the stock is sold. However, if he elected to receive the stock dividend, it is treated in the same manner as receipt of cash dividends; it's added to his investment income in accordance with the tax-paying rules described earlier in this chapter.

Consideration of the tax rules applicable to mutual funds and Dividend Reinvestment Plans (DRIPS) is beyond the scope of this chapter. We recommend that you consult a good tax book or an accountant to sort out these issues. For those up to the task, IRS Publication 550 (*Investment Income and Expenses*) and Publication 564 (*Mutual Fund Distributions*), as well as the section of the 1099-DIV form (*Capital Gains Distributions on 1099-DIV Forms*) are helpful resource guides.

Capital Gains and Losses

Throughout this book, we have stressed the importance of Teenvestors holding assets in their portfolio for the long term. Our basic goal has been to show Teenvestors how to make prudent and responsible investments. There may come a time, however, when your Teenvestor finds it necessary to sell assets in his portfolio. In the paragraphs below, we show how the profits (*capital gains*) or losses (*capital losses*) will be treated from a tax standpoint and reported on Schedule D (Form 1040). While the discussion below addresses capital gains and losses on stocks, we note that these concepts are generally applicable to mutual funds, bonds, and other assets.

The amount of tax owed on capital gains depends on the cost basis of the stock or other assets, how long the seller held the asset, and his income level. In order to determine the *cost basis* of stock, for example, it is necessary to know how the seller acquired the stock. If the Teenvestor purchased the stock through a custodial account, the cost basis is the purchase price plus commissions. If the stock is inherited, the cost basis is the fair market value of the stock at the date of the individual's death. If the stock was a gift, calculating the cost basis gets a little trickier. For our purposes, we need only note that in general, the cost basis of stock given as a gift is the donor's cost basis and, if the donor had to pay a gift tax, this is included as well. In addition, there are several ways to calculate the cost basis of mutual funds. We recommend that you consult a tax guide for more information in this area.

As most Teenvestors are in the 10% or 15% tax bracket, we will assume that this is your Teenvestor's tax bracket as well. However, as we noted earlier, if your Teenvestor is under 14 and has investment income over $1,400, his capital gains will be taxed at your (the parent's) rate.

Profit on the sale of a stock that was held for less than a year, also known as *short-term capital gains*, will be taxed at your Teenvestor's ordinary income tax rate of 10% or 15%. Profits on the sale of a stock that was held for more than a year but less than 5 years, also known as *long-term capital gains*, will be taxed at 10% for Teenvestors in either tax bracket. Finally, profits on the sale of stock that was held for more than 5 years, are taxed at a rate of 8%. When trying to determine the holding period, the clock starts ticking from the date that the purchase order was executed, also known as the *trade date*, as opposed to the date that the securities appeared in your Teenvestor's account, also known as the *settlement date*. As you can clearly see, the longer your Teenvestor holds assets in his portfolio, the lower his tax liability.

If your Teenvestor sells stock at a loss (capital loss), the loss can be offset, dollar for dollar, against any capital gains that he might have. If his capital losses are more than his capital gains, he can claim a capital loss deduction on his tax return. The amount of the deduction that he can claim is the lesser of $3,000 or the actual amount of the loss. If you report your Teenvestor's losses on your (the parent's) return, the deduction is the lesser of $3,000 ($1,500 if you are married and file separately) or the actual amount of the loss your Teenvestor's capital loss and yours as well, if you have any.

On our website, www.teenvestor.com, you will find more information on taxes and on investments such as IRAs and college savings plans.

22

THE TEENVESTOR TEN

This chapter tells the results of our analysis of the various investment websites available on the Internet. Admittedly, personal judgment comes into play here but we also had some young people look at the sites to see whether they could get the information on stocks and mutual funds they were seeking from them. Our lists were compiled based on the opinions of these young people and on our own feelings as to the usefulness of the information provided by the websites. The best sites received The Teenvestor Ten Award for education, research, current business news, and online brokers.

Features offered by financial websites change from time to time. In addition, new websites that provide better information can show up overnight. For these reasons, The Teenvestor Ten list will change from time to time. Please check our website for adjustments to our lists.

As a first step in choosing Teenvestor-friendly websites, we eliminated sites that charge Teenvestors for accessing information. In addition, we eliminated sites that required too much personal information of the user, and sites that were too difficult to use or were simply too cluttered.

On our site, www.teenvestor.com, you will find links to the companies that made The Teenvestor Ten list in the four categories. These links will point you to the relevant sections on the sites of The Teenvestor Ten companies.

EDUCATION

Before a Teenvestor even begins to buy stocks or mutual funds, she must understand basic investing principles. This book is a start, but there are lots of educational materials available on the Internet. Most of them will do for your purposes. However, we first looked around for substantive sites that were specifically written for Teenvestors. Then we moved on to the sites for the beginning investors.

Needless to say, we think our site, www.teenvestor.com, is the most comprehensive teen investment education site there is. Our website also gives numerous links to other websites to help you along the way and lists organizations that can help young people learn more about investing. And the bonus feature on our site is that it includes a young entrepreneur's section as well. All in all, www.teenvestor.com should be your first stop when you begin your investment journey. Here are The Teenvestor Ten Educational Websites:

The Teenvestor Ten (Education Websites)

Teenvestor.com	www.teenvestor.com
TeenAnalyst.com	www.teenanalyst.com
The Motley Fool	www.fool.com
Investopedia.com	www.investopedia.com
Morningstar.com	www.morningstar.com
NASD Individual Investor Services	www.investor.nasd.com
Individual Investor	www.individualinvestor.com
InvestorGuide.com	www.investorguide.com
SmartMoney	www.smartmoney.com
The Vanguard Group	www.vanguard.com

RESEARCH

A Teenvestor must do her own research before investing in any stocks or mutual funds. This research need not be difficult if she goes to the right websites. We found that some research sites were too difficult to use. To be sure, most of them provide the same types of information, but some were better organized than others. In addition, we found that too many sites assumed an advanced knowledge of the market.

Although we feel that a Teenvestor can muddle through any research site and eventually get the information she needs, we decided to include on our list, the best-organized websites and the websites that beginning investors can truly use with ease. Some of the criteria we used in determining our top research websites included the availability of the following information: stock quotes (historical graphs are a plus), company descriptions, industry comparisons, earnings data (historical PE ratios, EPS, ROE, etc.), earnings growth rates, market capitalizations, balance sheets and other financial information. Here are The Teenvestor Ten Research Websites:

The Teenvestor Ten (Research Websites)

Multex Investor	www.multexinvestor.com
MSN MoneyCentral Investor	www.moneycentral.msn.com
Hoover's Online	www.hoovers.com
Smart Money	www.smartmoney.com
Morningstar.com	www.morningstar.com
The SEC	www.sec.gov
Zacks.com	www.zacks.com
Netstockdirect	www.netstockdirect.com
FreeEDGAR	www.freeedgar.com
InsiderTrader.com	www.insidertrader.com

CURRENT NEWS ABOUT COMPANIES

The research sites in the previous section often have recent articles about public companies. But we find that it is sometimes better to go to websites that specialize in gathering news on a daily basis for up-to-date information on these companies. Here are The Teenvestor Ten Current Business News Websites:

The Teenvestor Ten (Current Business News Websites)

CBS Market Watch	www.cbsmarketwatch.com
CNBC.com	www.cnbc.com
CNNfn.com	www.cnnfn.com
TheStreet.com	www.thestreet.com
Yahoo!Finance	www.yahoo.com
PersonalWealth.com	www.personalwealth.com
New York Times	www.nytimes.com
Business Week Online	www.businessweek.com
Bloomberg.com	www.bloomberg.com
Quote.com	www.quote.com

ONLINE BROKERS

Online brokers offer investors a lot on their sites to entice them to sign up. They even add a lot of educational and research material just to get you to become informed enough about the stock market so that you are comfortable buying shares through them. However, we take a simplified approach to online brokers because we don't really care about all the "bells and whistles" they offer to investors. We just want to know whether Teenvestors can primarily buy stocks cheaply through them (using custodial accounts) without holding big cash balances in their investment accounts. All other considerations, such as getting "real-time" stock quotes as opposed to stock prices delayed be 15 minutes, should be of no real concern to the Teenvestor who just wants to invest whatever little money she has in the stock market for a long period of time. Here now are The Teenvestor Ten Online Brokers:

The Teenvestor Ten (Online Brokers)	
BuyandHold	www.buyandhold.com
ShareBuilder	www.sharebuilder.com
Firstrade	www.firstrade.com
Trading Direct	www.tradingdirect.com
Mydiscountbroker.com	www.mydiscountbroker.com
Quick & Reilly	www.quickandreilly.com
Scottrade	www.scottrade.com
Datek	www.datek.com
Empirenow.com	www.empirenow.com
TD Waterhouse	www.tdwaterhouse.com

Index

Page numbers in **bold** indicate tables.